To Carole -

4

In Memory of Mary Florence -

ALL THINGS NEW

She loved reading these.

2021 – 2022

ALL THINGS NEW

2021 – 2022

Wayne E. Fowler

2023

Acknowledgment

Except where otherwise indicated, all Scripture quotations in this book are taken from The New American Standard Bible ®, Copyright © 1960, 1962, 1963, 1968, 1971, 1972, 1973, 1975, 1977, 1995 by the Lockman Foundation. Used by permission.

First Printing: 2023

ISBN 978-1-329-96536-2

Wayne E. Fowler
287 Crawford Road
Blairsville, GA 30512

www.mountainchristian.net

Available at www.lulu.com.

Contents

Foreword

This book is a collection of articles I originally prepared for the North Georgia News, Blairsville, Georgia during 2021 – 2022, as indicated by the date of publication noted with each title. These are also posted at www.mountainchristian.net.

The newspaper column is for pastoral topics. My goal is to inform, educate, challenge, inspire, and motivate believers and non-believers via theology, current events, history, politics, philosophy, arts, and literature, a tall order for short articles! My limitation was column length, so I apologize to the reader for the brevity and occasional lack of thoroughness and continuity.

I have included Scripture References and a topical Index for your use.

Thanks to my dear wife Laura who faithfully read each article and offered much-needed editorial comments. However, any errors remain my own.

*And He who sits on the throne said, "Behold, I am making **all things new**." And He said, "Write, for these words are faithful and true" (Rev. 21:5).*

WEF

No More Time

January 6, 2021

Each December when World magazine recaps the year, I turn to the list of deaths. Reading what people did or how they died reminds me I still have time. It also raises questions about the finite human experience.

I noticed a few entries on the list. NBA All-Star Kobe Bryant died in a helicopter crash. Actor Robert Conrad did his own stunts. Kenny Rogers is "The Gambler" no more. Ken Osmond played Eddie Haskell on "Leave It to Beaver." John Lewis marched with Martin Luther King, Jr. Herman Cain died with COVID. Justice Ruth Bader Ginsburg was known by her initials. Eddie Van Halen was a Rock and Roll guitarist.

The passing of time and people increases the stream of probing thoughts and demands some mental bandwidth. I'll borrow the questions that Leo Tolstoy said nearly drove him to suicide. "What will become of what I do today or tomorrow? Why do I live? Why do I wish for anything or do anything? Is there any meaning in my life that will not be annihilated by the inevitability of death?"

An awareness of the passing of time is a defining and sometimes alarming feature of the human experience. The year changes. A life passes. The mirror startles. An intrusive thought emerges - time never stops ticking along. You can't stop it or even slow it down. What you can do is make the most of your appointed time, however uncertain its boundaries may be. How? The One through whom all things came into being, the One who is life and light (John

1:4) is the source of transcendent and timeless human meaning. God created humans to know and glorify him. That has unique meaning for your life.

After his Resurrection, Jesus walked with two friends toward Emmaus. They didn't recognize him. As they approached the village, "They urged him saying, 'Stay with us, for it is getting toward evening and the day is now nearly over.' So he went in to stay with them" (Luke 24:29). While with them he revealed truth in a life-changing way. He infused their lives with clarity, meaning, and destiny because they had seen the One who died yet lives, the One who made time yet releases you from its restraints. He's also willing to walk and stay with you.

If the Lord tarries, your name and a brief description of your life could someday appear in a publication. People may read and learn a little about you. Your loved ones will remember you. Will they know that you walked with Jesus even as the evening time approaches? Did you travel this sod with God-given purpose? When the day is over and you no longer journey in the land of the dying, by faith in the Lord Jesus you will stay with him in the land of the living where time is no more.

Right Side of History

January 13, 2021

A U.S. physician became alarmed by his elderly mother's observations. She spoke from her experience resisting communism's early advances and suffering as a political prisoner in Eastern Europe. Rod Dreher recounts the story in his book, <u>Live Not By Lies</u>. Recent stories of cancel culture in the U.S. alarmed the lady and brought back buried memories. Not unlike the 20th century, a damaging ideology is pitched today as something good, even in a religious way. Don't be deceived.

Dreher describes it like this: "It masquerades as kindness, demonizing dissenters and disfavored demographic groups to protect the feelings of victims in order to bring about social justice. The contemporary cult of social justice identifies members of certain social groups as victimizers, as scapegoats, and calls for their suppression as a matter of righteousness." Unless you are one of the oppressed classes, you may not speak. It's about levers of power and redistribution of wealth. It even brands religious freedom as bigotry.

You cannot dismiss this as campus wokeness. It does exist in education, but also in politics, business, and the media. It brooks no dissent and divides people into two classes: oppressed and oppressor. It affirms its adherents in anything they feel or believe, even if it is self-destructive. It knows nothing of repentance and reconciliation, only retribution. It self-defines righteousness. It rejects the

3

basis of equality, that all people are created in God's image. Can such defects yield true justice? The prophet Habakkuk warned about injustice some 2600 years ago. "Strife exists and contention arises. Therefore the law is ignored, and justice is never upheld. For the wicked surround the righteous; therefore justice comes out confused" (Hab. 1:3-4).

So how do Christians face ideology that denies truth? Christianity is more than a set of beliefs and behaviors. It is more than a worldview. It is a relationship with the Creator who forms your new identity in Christ. We are people who love God and neighbor, as Jesus said. We face defective ideologies by trusting God's Providence to accomplish His purposes regardless of people who live as though he doesn't. "The righteous will live by his faith" (Hab. 2:4), not by hate, fear, or coercion. So, offer refuge and truth to those damaged by cultural lies. Forgive those who would cancel you because you do not live by their lies. "I will rejoice in the God of my salvation (not in this rising ideology.) The Lord God is my strength" (Hab. 3:18-19).

When enough people demanded truth and liberation in Eastern Europe, communism collapsed. History shows that the followers of Christ and His gospel outlasted it. The dark secrets of any modern ideology cannot remain hidden from the light of God's revealed truth. Side with your Creator and resist cancel culture, and you will be on the right side of history.

Boldly and Joyously

January 20, 2021

I have questions. Strange and unusual events lead me to this basic question, how now shall we live?

First let me clear away some current events questions I don't presume to answer. COVID emerged amid shocking warnings that it could be bad. Are economic shutdowns and personal isolation worse than the disease? Cities in the USA burned while authorities allowed lawless autonomous zones. Will that kind of territorial lawlessness reappear again or elsewhere?

Claims of election fraud persist from both sides of the aisle. Will Americans ever trust another election? When people stormed the capitol last week, did they really think anything good would come of it? Will Big Tech censor my speech if they disagree with my perspective? Mr. Biden promised to sign the Equality Act in his first 100 days. Will this Act make people of faith less equal because we believe the government should not force a disordered view of humanity on citizens?

Jesus' fisherman friend wrote to believers scattered in a culture that discriminated against them because of their faith (1 Peter). From that letter, here are five ways you can live now in today's world.

1. Love people. If you are obedient to the truth of Christ, then your soul has a new capacity to love people. Racism, envy, and strife are selfishness, not love. To "fervently love

one another from the heart" is to boldly proclaim Jesus, who even said to love your enemy! (1:22)

2. Remember who you are. You are an "alien and stranger," just passing through this world. Feeling anxious and disenfranchised comes from a desire for control, a worldly lust that wages war against the soul. An eternal perspective brings joy. (2:11)

3. Live an honorable life. If someone slanders you as evil because you fear God and apply his truth to life, respond boldly with "good deeds" and "excellent behavior." People notice that, and it glorifies God. (2:12)

4. Speak truth. Align your faith, deeds, and words by setting up Christ Jesus as Lord in your heart. As you live with the joy and hope you have in Christ, people will notice. Be prepared to boldly "give an account for the hope that is in you, yet with gentleness and reverence." Your hope is Jesus. Whoever believes in him will have eternal life. That's truth. (3:15)

5. Endure suffering with purpose. Do not be surprised at the fiery ordeal that tests and strengthens your faith. Jesus said you are blessed when this happens. "If you patiently endure it, this finds favor with God." Consider it all joy when you encounter various trials. (4:12, 2:20)

Chuck Colson's answer to the question, "How now shall we live?" is found in his book by that title. He writes, "By embracing God's truth, understanding the physical and moral order he has created, lovingly contending for that truth with our neighbors, then having the courage to live it out in every walk of life. Boldly and, yes. Joyously."

Peaceful Fruit

January 27, 2021

Deion Sanders is the only athlete who has played in a World Series and a Super Bowl. To what did that success lead him? Attempted suicide.

Sanders played in the 1992 World Series (Braves). He is a two-time Super Bowl champion (1994-49ers; 1995-Cowboys). Despite fame and fortune, in 1997 he drove his car off a 40-foot cliff. Intentionally. He writes in his biography, "I was going through the trials of life. I was empty, no peace, no joy." His soul warred with the fruitlessness of his life.

With Sanders, did God almost drop the ball? Is it God's job to ensure you have a nice life while you try to be a moral and successful person? That sounds religious, but it isn't Christianity. The Christian worldview makes sense of life as you experience it, and trials are part of everyone's experience. But trials do not tell your whole story.

Good can come from suffering. By it we can experience God's comfort and grace. Theologian J. I. Packer explains that the purpose of our troubles and perplexities "is to ensure that we shall learn to hold Him fast. When we are caught in rough country in the dark, with a storm getting up and our strength spent, and someone takes our arm to help us, we shall thankfully lean on him." When suffering finds you, walk it to the foot of the cross. There you'll meet the One who knows about suffering and gives you peace despite the human experience. That's the rest of the story.

7

Suffering teaches you to accept God's rule in your life. "It is through many tribulations that we must enter the kingdom of God" (Acts 14:22). Chuck Colson, who spent time in prison after Watergate, agrees. "God uses the thorns and thistles that have infested creation since the Fall to teach, chastise, sanctify, and transform us, making us ready for that new heaven and earth. The greatest blessings in my life have emerged from suffering. God's purposes are the context that give suffering meaning and significance."

Meaninglessness tortured Deion Sanders. But then he experienced this truth: "He disciplines us for our good, so that we may share His holiness. For the moment, all discipline seems not to be pleasant, but painful; yet to those who have been trained by it, afterward it yields the peaceful fruit of righteousness" (Heb. 12:10-11). Sanders said after the suicide attempt, "I finally just got on my knees and gave it all to the Lord. My faith is everything. It's the air that provokes me to live."

Now Sanders coaches young men at Jackson State University. He partners with Stand Together in Dallas to eradicate poverty and youth violence. Through the way of suffering, he has found the peaceful fruit of righteousness and offers it to others. Let that be your story, too.

Graceful Unity

February 3, 2021

At the presidential inauguration, country music artist Garth Brooks offered truth. It was as though "the fragrance of the knowledge of Him in every place" had been revealed (2 Cor. 2:14).

As a solo trumpet sounded the opening lines, Brooks removed his trademark cowboy hat. He sang, "Amazing grace, how sweet the sound that saved a wretch like me." The verse moves people. Is it because we are lost and blind, and we sense it? Is it because we know we need God's grace to save us from this long night of the soul? John Newton penned those words from his dark experience as a slave trader, but his wickedness is no more wretched than yours and mine, for all have sinned.

Brooks continued, lifting both hands skyward as he sang, "When we've been there 10,000 years...we've no less days to sing God's praise than when we first begun." It is the most recognized Christian hymn in the world. Its timeless and vital message is for all who have ears to hear.

Some would claim that message is unity. For sure, we are divided by vitriol passed as politics, fear fed by the media, and coarseness embraced by culture. Earlier in the week Brooks said, "The message they (politicians) are pushing is unity, and that's right down my alley, man." I guess that's why he asked everyone to sing along. I appreciate the sentiment, but that was a symbolic unity at best.

The push for unity can be deceptive. A call for political unity is usually a demand for the other side to capitulate. A call for religious unity ignores the exclusive truth claims of distinct religions. Calling for unity was not Jesus' method. In fact, he expected to be divisive (Luke 12:51). British theologian J. C. Ryle criticized false unity. "People cannot believe that any earnest, clever, and charitable man can ever be in the wrong. Peace without truth is a false peace…unity without the gospel is a worthless unity. Let us never be ensnared by those who speak kindly of it."

Yet a certain unity does exist and is attainable – a unity in truth. Jesus prayed, "The glory which You have given me I also have given to them, so that they may be one…I in them and you in me" (John 17:22-23). Paul tells how that happens. "For you are all sons and daughters of God through faith in Christ Jesus" (Gal. 3:26). Those who believe in the One who is Truth share the powerful unity of a loving family.

Newton's life and lyrics reflect amazing grace as told in Jesus' story of the prodigal. "This son of mine was dead and has come to life again; he was lost and has been found" (Luke 15:24). By faith you are found and raised to life in Christ. By faith you join the family of God and enjoy the hope of eternity. The sweet sound of that graceful unity is the right message for today.

A Stirring Reminder

February 10, 2021

Sometimes life reminds us to number our days. Death does too. It can stir you to consider what really matters.

Larry King died a few weeks ago. He told Conan, "I don't believe in an afterlife. I can't, I just never accepted it." I respect that, but it's sad. He continued, "The only hope, the only fragment of hope, is to be frozen and then someday, they cure whatever you died of, and you're back." Once King interviewed Billy Graham about his book <u>Facing Death and the Life After</u>. King asked, "What's on the other side?" Graham replied, "On the other side is heaven or hell. That's what the Bible teaches."

Graham ministered in non-religious, secular settings because Jesus sought out those settings, too. People wrestle with questions like King asked. King did not accept the clear answer offered by Jesus. "I am the resurrection and the life. Whoever believes in me, though he die, yet shall he live" (John 11:25). The evidence that Jesus lived after he died is far more reassuring than the "fragment of hope" that a frozen body might be thawed back to life someday.

Baseball great Hank Aaron died the day before Larry King. You may not realize how much hate Aaron had to endure even while Martin Luther King, Jr. reminded us of the "promissory note" of American freedom and equality. How did Aaron cope? He said, "I need to depend on Someone who is bigger, stronger, and wiser than I am. I don't do it on my own. God is my strength. He lights the way." About playing he said, "I felt like I was surrounded by angels, and I had God's hand on my shoulder." He had an assurance unknown to Larry King.

Who'll die next? In his typical dry wit, C. S. Lewis reminds those who fear death that "100 percent of us die, and the percentage cannot be increased." Likewise, the Bible says, "It is appointed for men to die once, and after this comes judgment" (Heb. 9:27). As you ponder that inevitability, these precious promises are such good news: "The free gift of God is eternal life in Christ Jesus our Lord" (Rom. 6:23) and "To live is Christ and to die is gain" (Phil. 1:21).

Thinking about his destiny Paul writes, "We are of good courage and prefer rather to be absent from the body and to be at home with the Lord" (2 Cor. 5:8). His friend Peter adds urgency. "I consider it right...to stir you up by way of reminder, knowing that the laying aside of my earthly dwelling is imminent" (2 Pet. 1:13-14). The reminder is that you must enter the eternal kingdom of our Lord and Savior Jesus Christ by faith before you lay aside your earthly dwelling.

If you are to be stirred up by life or death, let it be about things that ultimately matter. Such as your ultimate destiny.

Foolish Delusion

February 17, 2021

On a recent episode of "Real Time," Bill Maher repeated Sigmund Freud's charge that religion is "mass delusion." Maher has suggested before that science and thinking are opposed to faith. By framing faith as ignorant, he would convert you to his irreligion.

Here is his full quote. "The inconvenient truth here is that if you accord religious faith the kind of exalted respect we do here in America, you've already lost the argument that mass delusion is bad." He was criticizing delusional conspiracy theories and found a way to disparage Christians in the same breath. It's true that outlandish conclusions drawn from random facts and innuendo are not harmless. But that's not Christianity.

One of the foundational beliefs of Christianity is that God exists. Is that ignorant? To answer that, let's call British professor and philosopher Anthony Flew to the witness stand. As a longtime atheist he wrote, "It is impossible to establish the existence of God, or even to show that it is more or less probable." But in 2004, he courageously announced a change. He concluded the evidence of modern science indeed establishes the existence of God.

As a new deist Flew wrote, "Science spotlights three dimensions of nature that point to God. The first is the fact that nature obeys laws. The second is the dimension of life, of intelligently organized and purpose-driven beings, which arose from matter. The third is the very existence of nature." He also pointed to the DNA genome, saying "that it has shown, by the almost unbelievable complexity of the arrangements which are needed to produce life, that intelligence must have been involved in getting these extraordinarily diverse elements to work together." Thank you, Dr. Flew for recognizing the evidence for design and the logical inference that God exists.

I don't have space here to call witnesses to explore other logical evidence, such as the material universe requiring an immaterial first cause and the impossible odds that the precise parameters necessary to sustain life made an unguided appearance in the universe. I will pose these questions for your consideration: How is it we all have an innate sense of morality, i.e., how could a material universe that "is" produce within sentient beings a sense of what "ought" to be? Why ignore the historical evidence that the Resurrection of Christ actually happened?

The Bible anticipates discussions like this. It says, "For since in the wisdom of God the world through its wisdom did not come to know God, God was well-pleased through the foolishness of the message preached to save those who believe" (1 Cor. 1:21). Vocal and influential people may claim to be wise and knowledgeable, while canceling God talk as foolish. Yet that "foolishness" contains the keys to answering the ultimate questions of origin, meaning, morality, and destiny. One wonders who is delusional, Mr. Maher.

Nature's God

I have found that the most inspiring use of social media is to enjoy the beauty of creation in photos posted by friends. They see, they admire, they share. Simple formula. I have done the same.

Here is what I have seen. The ancient Appalachians frame horses and green pastures. Hikers on high hills marvel at rock formations and unusual flora. Soaring reds and lavenders trail the setting sun promising, "I'll see you on the other side." Today's warmth lays aside for tomorrow's gentle snow. Green holly is bejeweled in red and capped in white. Now do the daffodils awake so soon? The hungry honeybee considers the humble henbit's purple blossom her royal feast.

I'm no poet, but the Creator is and nature is His scroll. He beckons you to see what He has done, and marvel. The Bible says, "Since the creation of the world His invisible attributes, His eternal power and divine nature, have been clearly seen, being understood through what has been made, so that they are without excuse" (Rom. 1:20). If you look at nature and marvel, then you know enough about God to honor him as God.

George Washington Carver certainly did. He said, "I love to think of nature as an unlimited broadcasting station, through which God speaks to us every hour, if we will only tune in." Carver was born into slavery in

Missouri. He became the first black student at Iowa State in 1891 and earned two degrees in agriculture.

As a longtime researcher at Tuskegee Institute, he found alternatives to cotton which was depleting the soil. He developed hundreds of products from peanuts and sweet potatoes. He told of his inspiration. "When I was young, I said to God, 'God, tell me the mystery of the universe.' But God answered, 'That knowledge is reserved for me alone.' So I said, 'God, tell me the mystery of the peanut.' Then God said, 'Well George, that's more nearly your size.' And he told me."

Carver came to faith as a child. He saw a boy walking to Sunday School. "I asked him what prayer was and what they said. I do not remember what he said; I only remember that as soon as he left I climbed up into the loft, knelt down by the barrel of corn and prayed as best I could. That was my simple conversion." That's the story of the esteemed professor who found beauty in creation and truth in its Creator. Do likewise, and you will have something inspiring to share with your friends!

"When I consider Your heavens, the work of Your fingers, the moon and the stars, which You have ordained; what is man that You take thought of him, and the son of man that You care for him?" (Psa. 8:3-4).

Shoveling Love

March 3, 2021

LA Times columnist Virginia Heffernan received some pushback from her readers. She wrote about her neighbors shoveling snow from her driveway without her asking. She labeled what they did "aggressive kindness."

She rejected their act of neighborly service because she despises them for their politics. She compared their act of neighborliness to Hezbollah doing someone a favor or Nazis being polite. That over-the-top comparison is why pundits hit her. She also stated the obvious: "Loving your neighbor is evidently much easier when your neighborhood is full of people just like you."

Her struggle is actually with loving her "enemy," a startling ethic taught by Jesus. "Love your enemies and pray for those who persecute you so that you may be sons of your Father who is in heaven." He included that in his call to perfection, a very high bar indeed (Matt. 5:44ff). How are we to do that?

It helps to realize God loved you before you were ever aware of him, and while you were a spiritual orphan. "How great a love the Father has bestowed on us, that we would be called children of God" (1 Jn. 3:1). God's love is empowering. "We love, because He first loved us" (1 Jn. 4:19). C. S. Lewis explains that the Divine gift to man "enables him to love what is not naturally loveable; lepers, criminals, enemies, morons, the sulky, the superior and the sneering."

17

That empowering love not is not a feeling or speaking, but a doing. "Let us not love with word or with tongue, but in deed and truth" (1 Jn. 3:18) and that includes enemies. Who is your enemy, anyway? Maybe someone despises you for your politics or religion. Maybe your "intersectionality" score is low. Jesus didn't directly address that question, but he did answer this: "Who is my neighbor?"

Jesus told the story of a man who did what the religious people wouldn't. This man, hated for his ethnicity, helped the victim of a highway robbery. He did it at great sacrifice to himself. This Good Samaritan story illustrates Jesus' charge to love your neighbor. He showed that your neighbor may be a stranger or even an enemy who despises you. Either way, to love is to be like God who loved you first.

Heffernan's neighbor may have committed his act of driveway aggression after hearing Sen. Ben Sasse calling for an end to political feuding. Sasse said, "You can't hate someone who shovels your driveway." The corollary is that it's easier to love someone when you are shoveling their driveway. It's sacrificial. It's in their interest. And that's why it is God-like.

To love like God loves you is to sacrifice on behalf of others, putting their interests before yours. Know when to be generous. Allow yourself to be inconvenienced. Listen more than you speak. Do not let disagreements about religion or politics stop you from being kind. And maybe you shovel your neighbor's driveway.

Healing Words

March 10, 2021

*See how great a forest is set aflame by such a small fire!
And the tongue is a fire, the very world of iniquity...(It)
sets on fire the course of our life, and is set on fire by hell.
(Jas. 3:5-6)*

Smith College is an elite women's liberal arts college in Massachusetts. It is suffering from too much attention lately, including a recent article in the New York Times.

Cafeteria worker Jackie Blair worked on campus at a camp for children during the 2018 summer term. One day when a college student entered the cafeteria, Blair mentioned that it was reserved for the children. The student ignored her and took food to a nearby lounge area. A janitor saw the student in the closed dorm and notified campus police per protocol. The officer made brief contact with the student but took no action.

That evening the offended student posted on social media, "It's outrageous that some people question my being at Smith." She claimed racial profiling and gender bias. She "doxed" Blair and a janitor who wasn't there. Her words set the world on fire.

The college put the janitor on leave. They initiated police sensitivity and staff anti-bias training. During that training, Jodi Shaw refused to accept the premise that she is inherently privileged and biased because of her race.

19

She resigned and may sue the school as a hostile workplace, an ironic twist.

Blair has been harassed by major media outlets. After being turned down for a job she said, "What do I do? When does this racist label go away?" Recently retired colleague Tracey Culver said, "We were gobsmacked – four people's lives wrecked. How do you rationalize that?" A law firm investigated on behalf of the college and found no evidence of bias during the incident. While the original offense never happened, the Times insisted the student's deeply felt personal truth mattered more than facts.

I have no interest in taking sides here, but I do see this as an example of the power of words. They can tear down, set afire, and deceive. Or they can encourage, edify, and reveal. Speak quickly and you will say the most impactful words you will ever regret. Slow down, manage your emotions, and consider whether your words are true, kind, and necessary, and then your words will be wiser.

The world today is complicated by social and moral upheaval, but how you speak to it is not. Consider the simple lesson from Sunday School:

O be careful little tongue what you say!
For the Father up above is looking down in love.
So, be careful little tongue what you say!

"There is one who speaks rashly like the thrusts of a sword, but the tongue of the wise brings healing" (Prov. 12:18). Speak healing words.

The Narrow Way

March 17, 2021

I have a Georgia Peach Pass. That means I can exit the busy freeway through the toll gate and use the single lane that skips past the notorious Atlanta congestion. I might admit to a little survivor's guilt when I see the hapless souls stuck with the trucks, going nowhere.

It reminds me of something Jesus said. "The gate is small and the way is narrow that leads to life, and there are few who find it" (Matt. 7:14). It's not the small gate and narrow way that alarm me. It's the "few who find it" part. He also said, "Strive to enter through the narrow door; for many, I tell you, will seek to enter and will not be able" (Luke 13:24). He went on to describe people knocking on a door claiming with futility that the head of the house should know them.

Why is the portal to the truest expression of human life, living in communion with God, hard to find? In a bit of irony, the answer for some is God's common grace. You experience the beauty of creation, the love of family and friends, or success in your endeavors and things seem right with the universe. When life feels right, you might fail to realize that something is wrong between you and God.

In <u>Screwtape Letters</u>, C. S. Lewis imagines comments by a devilish tempter whose enemy is God. Screwtape says, "The only thing that matters is the extent to which you separate the man from the Enemy (God). It does not matter how small the sins are, provided that their

21

cumulative effect is to edge the man away from the Light...Indeed, the safest road to Hell is the gradual one – the gentle slope, soft underfoot, without sudden turnings, without milestones, without signposts." Indeed, the wide gate and broad road represent the comfortable, autonomous way of life. That's a disconcerting thought.

But all is not lost. Once, people asked Jesus, "Who can be saved?" He responded, "With people this is impossible, but with God all things are possible" (Matt. 19:26). God has made a way when there seems to be no way. To be specific, Jesus said, "I am the door; if anyone enters through Me, he will be saved" (John 10:9). He is the small door. He said, "I am the way, and the truth, and the life; no one comes to the Father but through Me" (John 14:6). He is the narrow way.

The neighboring states of Florida and North Carolina welcome Peach Pass holders to travel those privileged lanes. It is good to know that the way to travel is open to you. It is good to find the way, even if it is narrow.

Prayer: Our Father in heaven, lead me to turn from my own way, to know the Way, and to walk in Him.

Effective Follower

March 24, 2021

"Follow the science!" is the cry of parents who have lost their patience with school districts in America yet to resume in-person learning. They have heard that the CDC has given a green light to open schools closed by the COVID pandemic.

The CDC published guidance that "presents a pathway to reopen schools and help them remain open through consistent use of mitigation strategies." It also says, "As science and data on COVID continue to evolve, guidance and recommendations will be updated to reflect new evidence." I appreciate the recognition that science isn't "settled" in this case. In fact, science often overrules previous conclusions based on new evidence. So, to "follow the science," you need to be somewhat circumspect.

The human effort via science to understand our world has yielded fascinating and powerful results. It has provided discoveries and inventions that affect many aspects of our lives. Yet science does not and in fact cannot have all the answers. Take the COVID vaccine, for example. Science may answer the question of how to prevent this infection. But science cannot answer who ought to be the first to receive immunization. That is a moral question, one lost on the people who finagled a way to jump ahead of nursing home residents and healthcare personnel. They followed the science, right to the front of the line.

Floating around in the minds of people today is the worldview that the universe began with a spontaneous, self-caused event which produced our solar system. Over millions of years, life fermented from a broth of ancient oceans and evolved to what we see today. With such unintentional origins, it follows that you can decide your morality and control your destiny. So why not jump to the front of the line, following your pre-determined desires?

On the other hand, if God created you then He has the answers about life and morality. Science, then, becomes one means to know the Creator as revealed in the physical world. The more science reveals the mysteries of creation, the more difficult it is to deny the Creator. Follow the science and behold the transcendent! Professor John Lennox writes, "There is an intelligent God who created, ordered and upholds the universe. He made human beings in his image...endowed with the capacity not only to understand the universe but to enjoy fellowship with God."

The Bible says that by Jesus "all things were created, both in the heavens and on earth, visible and invisible - through Him and for Him" (Col. 1:16). To enjoy fellowship with Him, answer His call to "Follow Me!" Do that and you will experience the life of an effective follower.

"Great are the works of the Lord. They are studied by all who delight in them. Splendid and majestic is His work, and His righteousness endures forever." (Psa. 111:2-3).

Honest Love

March 31, 2021

Let us not love with word or with tongue, but in deed and truth. We will know by this that we are of the truth, and will assure our heart before Him. (1 Jn. 3:18-19)

Kim Scott was an executive with Google and other tech companies. She tells about hiring "Bob," a likeable guy with a stellar resume. Soon it was apparent he couldn't do the work. She and the rest of the team covered for Bob...for a while. She finally fired him. He reacted, "Why didn't you tell me? Why didn't anyone tell me? I thought you all cared." It was uncaring to let him think all was well.

Love embraces truth, and truth matters. For example, if it's true that God made you, then that truth matters. It defines you. Truth matters because this is a sin-marred world that is good at deception. It matters because you cannot be anything you identify yourself to be, and you'll ruin yourself trying. Isn't it loving to be honest about that?

This might be inside baseball, but I've witnessed a lack of loving honesty among those who claim to represent the Christian worldview. Is as though they realize that since the message of the cross really is scandalous, it's up to them to soften and modernize it.

The soft line is that if you try hard to do better, that's enough. Hope your good outweighs the bad. God knows you try to do right. The modern take is that if you interpret the Bible the "right" way and account for the current cultural mood, you'll see God actually blesses what used to be sin.

Here is some honest love. The Bible says you are a broken, lost sinner in need of a Savior. That's the scandal. You are not "basically good" but when God re-creates you in Christ, you do inherit His goodness. Your high calling is to live out that new identity. Transformed by the love of Christ, you don't excuse or bless sin; you abandon it. You flourish as a human by believing what God says about you and by being reconciled to God through Christ on His terms. Love embraces the whole truth and nothing but the truth, even if it is painful.

In the foreword to Brennan Manning's The Ragamuffin Gospel, Christian music artist Rich Mullins described the gospel of Christ as "the good news that, although the holy and all-powerful God knows we are dust, he still stoops to breathe into us the breath of life – to bring to our wounds the balm of acceptance and love." Living by that good news is the best antidote to a world untethered to reality. To know and speak the truth is honest love.

"Speaking the truth in love, we are to grow up in all aspects into Him who is the head, even Christ" (Eph. 4:15).

It Happened

April 7, 2021

The bodily Resurrection of Jesus Christ is celebrated as a focal point of the Christian faith. Skeptics dismiss it as a myth or metaphor.

I love my non-believing friends and offer here a few of the many reasons to consider the Resurrection a life changing, historical event. I appeal to the scientific method of abduction, which is what detectives do as they seek the most logical explanation of a non-repeatable past event.

Was Jesus even a real person that died like the Bible says? Consider secular sources. Josephus, a first-century Roman Jewish historian, wrote an account of Jesus' death by crucifixion. Tacitus, also a first century figure and a Roman senator, recorded that Jesus "suffered the extreme penalty during the reign of Tiberius at the hands of Pontius Pilatus." They had access to eyewitnesses and no reason to propagate a fictional account.

Maybe the disciples fabricated the Resurrection to save face? For this to work, they would need to remove the body. In fact, those who had Jesus killed circulated that story. But it's implausible due to security measures in place at the tomb. A fabrication is even more implausible when you consider that Jesus' followers would have known it was a lie, yet they stuck to their story despite suffering persecution and death because of it. Why die for a fabricated tale?

Were the appearances of Jesus hallucinations? The disciples were pragmatic working men, not dreamers. They had no expectation of a resurrection and were disillusioned, afraid, and confused – the wrong preconditions for hallucination. Also, science has yet to document a group hallucination, and Jesus appeared to groups multiple times. After His death, people touched Him and ate with Him. One time He even prepared their breakfast on the beach. I wish I had been there for that!

What is the most plausible explanation for the empty tomb? No one ever produced a body to refute a resurrection "hoax." Hallucination cannot explain the multiple and simultaneous sightings of the resurrected Jesus. Would a fabricated story transform frightened disciples into bold preachers of Christ's Resurrection, releasing a movement that changed the world? In Gunning for God, Professor John Lennox quotes Norman Anderson summarizing the evidence. "The empty tomb forms a veritable rock on which all rationalistic theories of the Resurrection dash themselves in vain." The verdict: it happened.

The Bible offers you a challenge. Prove that the physical, bodily Resurrection of Jesus Christ did not happen, and you disprove Christianity. It says, "If Christ has not been raised, then our preaching is vain, your faith also is vain" (1 Cor. 15:14). The question that remains is, will you follow the evidence?

Culture Shifts

April 14, 2021

Wall Street markets were closed on Good Friday. Their other annual religious holiday is Christmas Day. Given the cultural trend toward a secular worldview, one wonders how long before they cancel or rename those holidays.

Just in my lifetime I've witnessed that trend. Growing up in the rural South, nothing was open on Sunday except churches and restaurants. I guess the city fathers didn't think the Lord would mind if we ate out after church meeting. Grandma was certain that fishing on Sunday was a sin, so we didn't. And we certainly had no little league baseball games or practice on the Lord's Day. Blue laws tended to keep things quiet one day a week so we could rest from our labors. Oh, the nostalgia of a sunny, lazy, Sunday afternoon with nothing to do, no place to go.

Times change. Gallop dropped a poll last week showing church membership among Americans fell below fifty percent for the first time, extending a 20-yr downward trend. Maybe that's why more businesses keep Sunday hours (but not a certain chicken chain based in Georgia).

Gallup attributes the church membership drop to (1) fewer Americans claiming any religious preference and (2) fewer religious Americans prioritizing church membership. The latter could be due to participation in religious activities in homes. Their tribe is increasing according to Barna Group, which estimates 12 million Americans attend a house church regularly.

In <u>The House Church Book</u>, Wolfgang Simpson writes, "The New Testament church was made up of small groups, typically between ten and fifteen people. It grew by multiplying 'sideways,' dividing like organic cells." The Bible mentions the church meeting in the homes of Aquila and Prisca (1 Cor. 16:19), Philemon and Apphia (Phile. 1:1-2), and others. Over time as the church gained influence it began to build sacred spaces, shifting away from home meetings.

While the culture shifts toward secularization and away from traditional values, many churches in America are strengthening their members with home fellowships. The last 30 years have proved their popularity, sometimes despite zoning threats against Christian friends meeting to pray. Some home gatherings are part of a traditional church, others function as churches. Maybe the church is experiencing its own cultural renewal, a return to our New Testament beginnings.

This time of year, Wall Street fears an old rumor that Good Friday trading led to the worst market collapse in history. Avoiding financial disaster is not the best reason to continue the Friday holiday. Some churchgoers believe a rumor that attending church tips the celestial scales in their favor. I can think of better reasons to gather with believers, like enjoying community and worship.

And what if that gathering is not in a religious building, but a house? Is that too much of a culture shift for you?

Christian Hope

April 21, 2021

"This increasing godlessness in America is actually a good thing, to be welcomed and embraced" (LA Times). Professor Phil Zuckerman believes progressive secularism offers hope.

He admits that religious organizations do good. "However, such welcomed charity is ultimately an altruistic response to symptoms," he says, "not a structural cure for root causes." He promotes secular efforts to address housing and healthcare issues. He believes secularism offers a better hope for human rights, environmental issues, and social justice.

I reverse these charges. Secular solutions do not recognize the basic problem. Humans are not "basically good" and just need more education or handouts. We are selfish, prideful, and yield to our base desires. Reckon with that root cause and your solutions will make more sense. Yet somehow the secular hope is that a sociologist or politician will usher in a better program to fix the human condition.

It's ultimately a worldview issue. Where is the hope if life is only material and limited by time? Where is the hope if we are all alone in a random, chaotic universe, and good and evil are just choices? Where is meaning in such a universe, if you deny the science that points to the metaphysical reality of a Creator God? Do you ever wonder how a mindless universe incapable of hope produces mindful, hopeful beings? A faulty worldview and its solutions address symptoms and cannot sustain hope.

But even a misplaced hope can teach you something. In Mere Christianity, C. S. Lewis writes about hope. When hope fails, you can blame the object of hope (politicians or programs), or "decide that the whole thing was moonshine!" (i.e., lower your expectations). Then he shows what misplaced hope teaches. "If I find in myself a desire which no experience in this world can satisfy, the most probable explanation is that I was made for another world...I must make it the main object of life to press on to that other country and to help others to do the same." Hope, even misplaced, points to the transcendent.

Christians find meaning and hope for life here and now because of our future hope. Paul reflects on the Resurrection of Christ and writes, "If we have hoped in Christ in this life only, we are of all men most to be pitied" (1 Cor. 15:19). Christians have hope imprinted on our souls. The hope Christ offers is that you are more than a physical body and are not alone. Meaning comes from following Jesus into the sufferings of humanity and loving your neighbor. The basic problem is human brokenness, but by faith your hope is in the One who loves you, makes you whole, and offers you eternity.

The hope of America and the world is Jesus Christ, not increasing godlessness. But I agree with Professor Zuckerman on this: we should not fear what's coming. Not because secularism has solutions, but because we Christians have hope.

May Day

April 28, 2021

The Soviet Union and Eastern Bloc governments adopted May 1 as a day to celebrate communism. They intended it to recognize laborers in their socialist system. They didn't know their governments would collapse under the weight of that system in less than 75 years.

China still celebrates the communist holiday to foster good will. If it is to survive, the Chinese Communist Party has to pacify the other 93% of Chinese citizens who are not Party members. The great con is that the Party is China's only hope for national survival and success.

A republic is not immune to a similar deception. The zeitgeist of recent years beckons you to trust politicians and government as your only hope. Why do people fall for that? In The Political Illusion (1967), Jacques Ellul writes about people acting with religious fervor for politics. They do not realize they're trying to address their own, unmet needs. He writes, "In great, solemn, vibrant meetings in defense of the republic man can experience the communion that he absolutely needs but no longer finds in his family, his neighborhood, or his work – a common objective, some great popular drive in which he can participate, a camaraderie, a special vocabulary, an explanation of the world. Politics offers him these joys and symbols." If politics is your source of identity and meaning, the bond that holds everything together, then you have traded your birthright for a bowl of lukewarm porridge. It's what mass media serves for dinner.

Where can you find the communion you need, something that explains the world and gives you meaning? Answers that fail to address what is true and real about the human condition, what's right and wrong, and ultimate destiny – they're porridge. It helps that Jesus gave us a simple outline for finding solutions. "Love the Lord your God" and "Love your neighbor as yourself" (Matt. 22:36-40). Paul repeated those ideas, declaring that his priority was "to know Him and the power of His resurrection" (Phil. 3:10) and that "love does no wrong to a neighbor" (Rom. 13:10).

Much of American politics today hurts and divides. It obscures the knowledge of the Creator and does wrong to people. Political posturing has infiltrated education, business, entertainment, and media. Yet we continue to endure the illusion that politics gives meaning and solves all problems. I borrow aviation's emergency call "Mayday" to appeal to heaven to deliver us from the crushing grip of that political illusion.

May Day is also a holiday about spring renewal and the release from winter's grip. May it be a time to renew your love of God and neighbor. Invest less energy in politics and more in your neighbors' well-being. Support your church's efforts to engage the local and global community. Put your trust not in government, but Providence who holds the nations in His hands.

Value of Motherhood

May 5, 2021

"Mom and apple pie." It was a common answer from WWII soldiers when asked, "What do you miss the most?" It led to the expression, "As American as motherhood and apple pie," a way to express values everyone accepts.

A scant 25 years after WWII, feminist Shulamith Firestone imagined a revolution leading to a motherless utopia. She wrote, "The goal must be the elimination of the sex distinction itself. The reproduction of the species by one sex for the benefit of both would be replaced by artificial reproduction: children would be born to both sexes independently of either. The dependence of the child on the mother would give way to dependence on a small group of others. The tyranny of the biological family would be broken." Even a casual observer can see the technological and cultural pieces of that vision emerging right now.

Truth is, many Americans reject this vision and its underlying values and wonder if their fellow citizens are capable of sorting truth from lies. There was a time most Americans would have agreed that the biological family is sacred, a gift meant for human flourishing. But now that's thrown back into the face of the Creator saying, "It's tyranny. I'll do it my way." After all, if a material universe spawned us by natural processes, why adhere to any "outdated" notions of man, woman, marriage, and family?

The beauty and value of motherhood and family are inherent in God's design. He created male and female in His image. He blessed them saying, "Be fruitful and multiply, and fill the earth." A man is to leave his father and mother and be joined to his wife, becoming one flesh. Eve conceived and gave birth to Cain saying, "I have gotten a manchild with the help of the Lord." (Gen. 1:27-28, 3:24, 4:1). God values mothers because they share in His creative work!

In the 1970's, Kamila Benda was a professor and mother in Prague, under communist rule. She devoted herself to preparing her children to resist the totalitarian lies, even after her husband became a political prisoner. She read stories to help them distinguish between truth and deception. Their favorite was <u>Lord of the Rings</u>. Rod Dreher asked her, "Why Tolkien?" She replied, "Because we knew Mordor was real. Resisting the evil Sauron was our story too" (see Dreher's book, <u>Live Not By Lies</u>). That her children kept the Christian faith to this day is a testament to their mother.

Despite a changing America, we still value Mom (and apple pie!). Mothers have had a key role in human flourishing since the beginning of time, and we still celebrate them with a holiday. So, thanking God for family and for the mother's love I have known, I value all mothers and wish you a happy Mother's Day!

A Senator's Redemption

May 12, 2021

U.S. Senator Tim Scott spoke to the nation last month. Even if you must set politics aside, you can appreciate his life story of hope and redemption.

Broadcasting to a national audience he said, "Growing up, I never dreamed I'd be standing here tonight. When I was a kid, my parents divorced. My mother, my brother, and I moved in with my grandparents. Three of us, sharing one bedroom. I was disillusioned and angry, and I nearly failed out of school. But I was blessed. First, with a praying momma. Then with a mentor, a Chick-fil-A operator named John Moniz."

Moniz had noticed and felt compassion for the young Scott. Motivated by his Christian faith, Moniz hoped to positively impact one million people. For four years he taught Scott the life lessons that had helped Moniz find success and significance. He wanted Scott to look beyond athletics and entertainment to more realistic goals, packaged as a "back-up plan." He said, "If you have a job you're doing well, but why not become a job creator?" Turns out that Scott needed a backup plan.

One evening while driving on the freeway, Scott fell asleep with his mother in the car. He awoke with a start and snatched the steering wheel. The car flipped and rolled into the opposing lane. They survived, but a broken ankle ended his big hopes for athletic success. He attended a small college where a fellow student, John

Rickenbacker, resumed the conversation that Moniz started. The result, Scott explains, was that in 1983 "I accepted Jesus Christ as the Lord of my life." He also implemented his backup plan, focusing on academics and entrepreneurship.

Scott sees God's sovereign hand in the near tragic accident and in the men who invested in him. When telling the story he recites, "We know that God causes all things to work together for good to those who love God, to those who are called according to His purpose" (Rom. 8:28). In Scott's story, that means an angry young man becomes a U.S. Senator, speaking to the nation.

Only four years after meeting Scott, Moniz died at age 38. But he did not fail in his goal to impact people. Scott's national audience far exceeded the number of people Moniz had hoped to impact, and they heard this uplifting message: "Original sin is never the end of the story. Not in our souls, and not for our nation. The real story is always redemption." I hear Moniz' voice loud and clear. Through the one he impacted his million, and more.

Some do the work of Christ as fast-food managers, some as students, some as redeemed senators, but all do it for the glory of God. "We are his workmanship, created in Christ Jesus for good works, which God prepared beforehand so that we would walk in them" (Eph. 2:10).

Praying for Liberty

May 19, 2021

Where the Spirit of the Lord is, there is liberty.
(2 Cor. 3:17)

The theme for this year's National Day of Prayer was, "Lord, pour out your love, life, and liberty." What an encouraging and timely prayer!

President Harry Truman inaugurated the National Day of Prayer in 1952. That same year, Paul Harvey wrote a book for Americans. He warned that fear is a tool to control people. He wrote, "man + fear − God = man over man." Almost 70 years later, politicians, media, and activists still mix fear and godlessness to accrue power. You may be aware of what's happening, but you don't have to respond in fear. Trust the presence of the Lord to give you freedom from fear. That is a liberty no one can take away.

The zeitgeist (cultural mood) of today entraps the soul. In The Rise and Triumph of the Modern Self, Carl Trueman writes that it "prioritizes victimhood, sees selfhood in psychological terms, regards traditional sexual codes as oppressive, and places a premium on the individual's right to define his or her own existence." Such a mood coerces people to create an identity, morality, and meaning *ex nihilo* (out of nothing). They're trying to build a smart phone with sand and a screwdriver. The good news is that God created with order and meaning, so when you discover His design and purpose for your life, you are liberated.

Another drain on freedom is unrestrained government. Levying usurious taxes, spending borrowed money, imposing overburdening regulations, removing the incentive to work, and funding the extermination of unborn humans are all forms of tyranny. The totalitarian impulse brands as a bigot anyone who speaks out to protect the innocent and preserve freedom. As government grows in power, we're reminded of Lord Acton's famous maxim "absolute power corrupts absolutely." The good news is that we know One who is more powerful and can displace tyranny and totalitarianism with liberty.

By far your greatest need for liberty is not from fear, culture, or government. You can suffer in a prison of sin without seeing the bars, but you can be set free! This is why the gospel is such good news! Jesus said the Father "has sent Me to proclaim release to the captive...to set free those who are oppressed." (Luke 4:18). Oppressed by what, you ask? He answers, "Everyone who commits sin is the slave of sin...so if the Son makes you free, you will be free indeed" (John 8:34, 36). Step into the sunlight of that freedom!

The National Day of Prayer is an important reminder that "God rules over the nations" (Psa. 22:28). But you don't have to wait for a special day to pray for liberty. Join me in praying that Americans experience the liberation they need, the freedom found only in Christ Jesus.

Enjoy His Presence

May 26, 2021

*He who has God and everything else
has no more than he who has God only. – C. S. Lewis*

How many friends or followers do you have on social media? Human nature compels you toward relationships. You want people to like your posts, know your name, and look at you when you enter the room. While it hurts to be ignored or considered irrelevant, you are gratified to be welcomed as part of the inner circle. That yearning, never fully satisfied by human relationships (or social media), points to something far more glorious.

In The Weight of Glory Lewis writes, "But we pine. The sense that in this universe we are treated as strangers, the longing to be acknowledged, to meet with some response, to bridge some chasm that yawns between us and reality, is part of our inconsolable secret. The promise of glory becomes highly relevant to our deep desire. For glory means good report with God, acceptance by God, and welcome into the heart of things." Nothing less than the presence of God is what we truly desire.

God created humans that way, and throughout history He met that need. He appeared to Adam and Eve, Abraham, and Moses. He was in the garden, the fiery furnace, and the temple. As the people returned to Jerusalem after their exile to Babylon, the Lord declared, "Behold I am coming and I will dwell in your midst. Many

41

nations will join themselves to the Lord in that day and will become My people" (Zech. 2:10-11). By this the Lord opened up the invitation to enjoy His presence.

He ultimately fulfilled the promise of His presence by stepping into His creation as Emmanuel, "God with us." He "became flesh and dwelt among us, and we saw His glory." His presence was not just for that moment. As Jesus told His disciples, "I will come again and receive you to Myself, that where I am there you may be also." He promised that the Father would send the Helper, the Spirit of truth, saying, "You know Him because He abides with you and will be in you." (Matt. 1:23, John 1:14, 14:3,17). God is present for you.

The writings of Brother Lawrence popularized "the practice of the presence of God." Awareness of God in each moment brings you peace, empathy, and contentment. It is an ongoing reminder that your identity and destiny are in Christ. Your awareness of the reality of God becomes apparent to the people around you as you live for the divine accolade, "Well done good and faithful servant."

As you travel through this life and gain relationships, remember the One who made your journey possible and prepared your ultimate destination. To have God is to have everything. Enjoy His presence.

Answer the Question

June 2, 2021

"If you were a tree, what kind of tree would you be?" Would you answer such a question?

Entertainment critics hit Barbara Walters hard for asking Katharine Hepburn a similar question on the "20/20" TV show in 1981. But the question wasn't random. Context helps. Hepburn complained that fame had made her into "sort of a thing." Walters asked, "What kind of thing?" Hepburn answered, "I'm like a tree," which elicited the follow up, "What kind of tree are you?"

Jesus used questions not to entertain, but to challenge his hearers to believe who He is. Consider these four questions recorded by John.

1. "What do you seek?" (John 1:38). Jesus directed this question to Andrew and John. At the time they were followers of John the Baptist who called Jesus "the Lamb of God." Were they looking for a different teacher to follow, or a stimulating religious talk? After spending the day with Jesus, Andrew told his brother Peter, "We have found the Messiah." Maybe the question helps you clarify what, or rather who, you seek.

2. "You are a teacher in Israel and you do not understand this?" (John 3:10). This was for Nicodemus, when he wondered how someone is born again of the Spirit. Jesus reminded him about Moses lifting the serpent on a pole to save the people. That event foreshadowed the Son of Man dying on the cross "so that whoever believes

43

will in Him have eternal life." Do you understand that Jesus is God the Son, and that His sacrificial death provides for you to be born again to eternal life?

3. "Do you believe this?" (John 11:26). Jesus asked Martha to believe her brother Lazarus would live again. He made the remarkable claim that "everyone who lives and believes in Me will never die." Do you believe Jesus not only raised Lazarus, but His own Resurrection was the miracle that authenticated everything He said?

4. "Because you have seen Me, have you believed?" (John 20:29). Thomas had been a doubter, wanting to see the resurrected Jesus for himself. Thomas touched Jesus just to make sure He was real. Then Jesus looked down through history and saw you. "Blessed are they who did not see, and yet believed," He said. Even though you have yet to see Him, do you still believe?

You can ignore a question. Hepburn might have dismissed Walters' question as too metaphorical. (She didn't. She saw herself as a "white oak tree, strong and great.") Maybe the person asking the question gives you pause. "May I take your pulse?" would be OK coming from your doctor, but weird from a co-worker. But when God takes on human flesh to read some questions into the historical record, they aren't metaphorical or weird. They're vital because of the Questioner and the question. So, give Him your answers.

Fruitful Abiding

June 9, 2021

I am the vine, you are the branches;
he who abides in Me and I in him, he bears much fruit,
for apart from Me you can do nothing. – Jesus

Ahead of me in line at the post office was a young mother with a toddler. An older woman couldn't help but chatting with the mom about the cute and active boy. As the conversation meandered, they touched in a lighthearted way on human foibles. Without hesitation the mom said, "Well, I'm so glad I have a forgiving Savior!" My heart leapt and I wished those further away in line could have heard that. Just then the older woman said, "I'm sorry, I didn't hear you?" Then the mom spoke it again, firmly and clearly for customers, clerks, God, and the angels to hear! Now you have heard it, too.

What does Jesus mean by bearing fruit? Is it not living with transparency about what ultimately matters and sharing that with fellow travelers? What is abiding, if not trusting Him to place you in a line at a post office at a particular moment and prompting you to speak? Moments like those add up to a lifetime of fruitfulness.

Martha Williamson became a Christian in 1981 a few years after beginning her career in Hollywood. She was an associate producer and aspiring writer but her earnest desire was for Jesus to bear fruit in her career. About her abiding lifestyle Chuck Colson writes, "She would do what

God put before her and let Him take her where she was meant to go. She believed that He knew the deepest desires of her heart and that He knew what He wanted for her. She would entrust everything to God's care."

Her big break came when CBS asked her to be the executive producer of a show with a religious theme. But she turned them down. It did not reflect what sincere people of faith believed. It was a silly caricature of spirituality. The day before her deadline to accept a job at another network, she woke up and realized God wanted her to stay at CBS. She gave up the sure job and took her pitch to CBS to rethink their religious show. They accepted her proposal.

The result was "Touched by an Angel," featuring Roma Downey and Della Reese. Every episode promoted the theme that God loves people and cares for those who are hurting. It followed the Biblical theme of angels as messengers. The show lasted nine seasons and continues to broadcast around the world in 60 languages. Williamson remains a fruitful Christian influence in Hollywood.

Whether in a Tinsel Town studio or a downtown post office, the Lord Jesus bears fruit in those who abide in Him. That is how you reflect the image of God imprinted on your soul.

Man of Prayer

June 16, 2021

George Muller (1805–1898) cared for over 10,000 orphans during his lifetime. He was a father to the fatherless because he saw his Heavenly Father answer prayer.

The plight of the orphan was a recurring theme for Muller's contemporary, Charles Dickens (think "Oliver Twist"). Dickens was so impressed with Muller's work for orphans that he wrote a 5000-word essay in his weekly journal ("Household Words," 1857) about "Brother Muller and his orphan work."

Dickens noted the remarkable role of prayer in Muller's life. One morning, Muller gathered the children for a breakfast without food. Just as they finished giving thanks for God's provision, the baker arrived with a donation of fresh bread. The milkman's cart broke down nearby, so he donated the milk. Muller never solicited funds or donations. He simply prayed for the Lord's provision and waited. Over his lifetime the cost of multiple orphan houses was the equivalent of millions of dollars in today's currency. Dickens wrote, "When he wants money, he prays for it. His reports make no appeal."

Jesus said, "What man is there among you who, when his son asks for a loaf, will give him a stone? Or if he asks for a fish, he will not give him a snake, will he? If you then, being evil, know how to give good gifts to your children, how much more will your Father who is in heaven give what is good to those who ask Him!" (Matt. 7:9-11). Even though you as a father can give in to the temptations of the human condition ("being evil") and do wrong by your children, you still want good things for them. The Heavenly Father loves your children and knows what they need. Jesus invites you to pray, and witness what the Father will do for them.

Do you pray for your children? You are far more motivated to pray when you contemplate the love and providence of God for you and your children. The One who created your children, the Son who sacrificed His life to reconcile them to God, the Spirit who comforts and guides, He is the One who invites your prayers. The all-powerful God invites you to have a front row seat as His will is done on earth as it is in heaven.

Your children live in a culture that encourages godless living and celebrates each doing what right in his or her own eyes. Pray they know the truth and the joy that accompanies those who walk with Jesus. Pray that God will orchestrate the circumstances of your children's lives so that they have an anchor for their souls in such a time as this.

What does George Muller's life say to fathers? It is the man of prayer who can best love, support, and guide the children in your life.

Rebuke the Winds

June 23, 2021

Fear is part of the human experience. It motivates us to act in ways that in hindsight we wish we hadn't. It's even worse if it reveals something important is lacking.

The word "fear" appears almost 400 times in the Bible, describing a range of human situations. In one account, we see a reaction to astraphobia (fear of storms). Late one evening, some men were in a small boat. Jesus was with them, asleep. A great storm arose over the sea, and they woke him. "Save us, Lord; we are perishing!" they cried. He admonished, "Why are you afraid, you men of little faith?" This was early in his earthly ministry and people were still learning about Him. He did rebuke the winds that night. "What kind of man is this?" they marveled (Matt. 8:24-27).

Fear moves in when faith is lacking. Many human fears, regardless of their fancy phobia words, are grounded in the fear of the unknown. Those men didn't know how bad the storm would become. They didn't know their chosen role in revealing God's plan in that moment. They didn't know how much Jesus loved them even amidst hardship. They didn't know God the Son was in the boat with them. He rebuked the winds that night because He meant for them to know Him and learn to trust Him.

The most powerful antidote to fear is knowing the love of God. "God is love, and the one who abides in love abides in God, and God abides in him. By this, love is perfected with us...There is no fear in love; but perfect love casts out fear" (1 Jn. 4:16-18). Anything else is an inferior antidote to fear. C. S. Lewis wrote, "It is very desirable that we should all advance to that perfection of love in which we shall fear no longer; but it is very undesirable, until we have reached that stage, that we should allow any inferior agent to cast out our fear." Those inferior agents may mask fears, but they don't rebuke them.

Three years later, those men knew much about Jesus' purpose and love. Under threat of imprisonment and death for talking about Jesus they declared to the authorities, "We must obey God rather than men" (Acts 5:29). Faith moved by love made them fearless.

If the God of the universe can reconcile you to Himself by His death on the cross, then His providential love can overcome fear of the unknown, even fear of death. You know your destiny. Jesus went to prepare a place for you, and it's a place of love that no uncertainties in this life can take away. Knowing Him, you can stand firm in your faith, abide in God's love, and rebuke the winds of fear.

The Perfect Result

June 30, 2021

I sat alone on the sidewalk outside the Port-au-Prince airport. My first trip abroad - and I was stranded. I didn't speak the language. Cell phones didn't exist. No one answered the one telephone number I had.

Four hours earlier when my ride hadn't appeared, a friendly American had pity and took me to a guest house. It was closed. I asked her to take me back to the airport. "It's closed, too, and there are no hotels or restaurants out there!" she protested. Against common sense, I insisted. We pulled up to the airport and I got out. I thanked her for the hour-long round trip while trying to avoid the look on her face. She drove away. Gone were the shouting people, clanking vehicles, roaring planes, and overpowering exhaust fumes. I only heard sparrows chirping as they hopped along the sidewalk tilting their heads at me. I might be sleeping outdoors tonight.

About 20 minutes after I arrived at the airport for the second time, a lone vehicle turned toward the terminal and pulled up beside me. "Are you Wayne?" the man asked. Keith was my tardy driver, and we became fast friends. I was to shadow him for a few days to consider an assignment developing drinking water sources in rural Haiti.

The next day we set out for a remote village. We drove toward the Artibonite River then continued on foot. The sun was intense, and the rainy season humidity was stifling. I huffed to keep up with the fit, former Army officer. We arrived at the launch for our river crossing. Our ride was a hollowed-out log with just enough room for the two of us, the boatman, and a man with a nervous yearling steer. I loosened my boot laces in case I had to swim. On the other side, we resumed our trek past gardens mounded with peanuts and potatoes, mud huts with thatched roofs, and dried corn hanging by the shucks above the reach of rodents. Keith procured two green coconuts so we could re-hydrate.

By day's end, I was sun burnt and exhausted with blistered feet. But exhilarated! The next season of life was now much less mysterious. It was an endurance test, but ultimately one of faith. "Consider it all joy, my brethren, when you encounter various trials, knowing that the testing of your faith produces endurance. And let endurance have its perfect result, so that you may be perfect and complete, lacking in nothing" (Jas. 1:2-4).

I returned to the airport at the end of that week astonished at how God in His Providence leads us through trials. By enduring those trials, you learn that God's grace is sufficient for you, that He is for you and with you. You can consider it all joy because your faith is more complete. That is the perfect result.

Washington's Prayer

July 7, 2021

At the end of the Revolutionary War, George Washington's desire was to retire to his estate on the Potomac River. I can see why. Mount Vernon is situated on a picturesque and productive tract of land, quite suitable for a retired soldier and gentleman farmer.

In his 1783 letter to the governors of the states resigning as commander of the continental army, he expressed hope for the country's future. He wrote that his prayer was that Americans would "demean ourselves, with that charity, humility, and pacific temper of mind, which were the characteristics of the Divine Author of our blessed Religion, and without an humble imitation of whose example in these things, we can never hope to be a happy Nation."

In modern English, he was saying that for the new country to work, its citizens must act toward each other with the love, humility, and peace that Jesus modeled. For the lives of 25,000 American soldiers not to be lost in vain, the new nation must succeed. To that end he believed we would do well to imitate Jesus. America still needs that mindset, and Christians can lead the way.

Jesus loved by caring for poor, disenfranchised, and suffering people. Government social programs are no substitute for that kind of love. Christians still do heavy lifting in this area and do it with a personal touch. Jesus also loved by telling the truth. American culture is courting destructive ideologies and Christians must speak the truth in love, and not repeat popular deceptions.

Jesus, God the Son, showed humility by stepping into the world He made. He put others before Himself, even unto death on the cross. Christians model humility by seeing the value of every person and respecting all people as God's image-bearers. Not every disagreement is an argument that must be won. "With humility of mind regard one another as more important than yourselves" (Phil. 2:3).

We need a peaceful state of mind. Jesus lived a peaceful lifestyle motivated by a higher purpose. Through Him we are reconciled to, and have peace with God. We are also reconciled to one another (Eph. 2:14ff). Racial, political, and interpersonal strife cannot coexist with the peace of Christ.

Washington wrote, "I bid a last farewell to the cares of office and all the employments of public life." Six years later, he consented to be the first President of the United States under the new constitution. If there is a lesson in his change of heart it is that a citizen's duty is never done. Even more, a Christian's duty is never done because our fellow citizens will always benefit from the love, humility, and peace that we have through Christ Jesus.

"Holy and beloved, put on a heart of compassion, kindness, humility, gentleness and patience; bearing with one another, and forgiving each other" (Col. 3:12-13).

Keeping Freedom

July 14, 2021

The recent fireworks celebrating Independence Day has me dwelling on the state of affairs in America. Not current events, but the state of our thinking about the underpinnings of our freedoms. Here's my hypothesis: Christianity can exist without freedom, but American freedom cannot exist without Christianity.

Let's dispense with the first part. Christianity is growing rapidly in China and North Korea, which do not allow freedom of speech, association, and religion. Christianity is expanding in the Middle East, a reaction to the more oppressive forms of Islam. The number of Christians in Iran has grown from five hundred to one million since the beginning of the Islamic Revolution. They certainly don't have American-style freedoms.

As for the second part of my hypothesis, American freedoms depend on Christian morality. Here are supporting thoughts from three non-believers.

Agnostic political scientist Charles Murray believes America needs a religious revival. He says, "Highly secular societies are going to break down. If you could have a resurgence of what used to be known as a religious Great Awakening — we've had three of them at least, maybe four — those had very good effects. Those could change the behavior of the population in very positive ways. And that's going to be great if that happens. If you have a new upper class that joins in a resurgence of the Judeo-Christian traditions, the United States could be great."

Stanford University professor Niall Ferguson says, "I was brought up as an atheist. It is as much a faith as Christianity. I've come to see as a historian that you can't base a society on that. Indeed, atheism, particularly in its militant forms, is really a very dangerous metaphysical framework for a society. I'm a big believer that with the inherited wisdom of a two-millennia old religion, we've got a pretty good framework to work with."

Atheist Richard Dawkins likes to quote Hillaire Belloc's poem for children. "Always keep a-hold of Nurse for fear of finding something worse." Dawkins' point is that an escaping child is to her caregiver what a godless country is to freedom. Both risk losing what they need most. Dawkins wants Christianity not because he believes it's true, but because nations need a moral underpinning.

America is afflicted these days with unrestrained people who "professing to be wise...became fools" (Rom. 1:22). They cannot see that "righteousness exalts a nation, but sin is a disgrace to any people" (Prov. 14:34). Fortunately, even non-believers recognize foolishness when they see it, and prefer a righteous nation that benefits from its Christian underpinnings. Truth is, America needs Christianity far more than Christianity needs America.

Benjamin Franklin once said America is "a republic, if you can keep it." We keep our republic free by being a moral people, one nation under God.

Honest Unbelief

July 21, 2021

If you do not identify as a Christian, have you ever thought about why you don't? Perhaps you haven't thought about it at all. Please give me a minute to challenge you about that.

Maybe you're like the non-believer I heard about who responded on social media to the disconcerting things happening today. He said, "I'm coming out. I'm officially Bible-curious." That's honest truth-seeking. Only God knows what makes a seeker out of a skeptic or cynic. A skeptic is unsure what is true; a cynic is not interested in what is true. You can be either or both. You can also be changed.

You live by what you believe is true whether you realize it or not. Consider the following popular truth claims: People are basically good. All paths lead to god. Nature is god. Science has all the answers. The cosmos is all that is or was or ever will be. Follow your heart. Since people wrote the Bible, their thoughts are no better than mine. Jesus is a mythical figure. Believing any of these would contribute to living by something other than the truth God has revealed.

You may object, "If Christianity is true, why doesn't everyone see and embrace it?" The answer lies at the heart of the Christian gospel. Humans are good at deceiving ourselves. St. Augustine wrote, "Because man hates to be proved wrong, he will not allow himself to be convinced that he is deceiving himself. So, he hates the real truth for what he takes to his heart in its place." You can find evidence for the real truth about God in history, science, logic, and changed lives.

Since "the heart is more deceitful than all else" (Jer. 17:9), the solution is what the Bible calls being "saved." It says, "He saved us, not on the basis of deeds which we have done in righteousness, but according to His mercy, by the washing of regeneration and renewing by the Holy Spirit, whom He poured out upon us richly through Jesus Christ our Savior, so that being justified by His grace we would be made heirs according to the hope of eternal life" (Tit. 3:5-7).

To be saved means that "you lay aside the old self, which is being corrupted in accordance with the lusts of deceit, and be renewed in the spirit of your mind, and put on the new self, which in the likeness of God has been created in righteousness and holiness of the truth" (Eph. 4:22-24). It means you have a new identity!

How do you embrace the grace, forgiveness, renewal, and eternity the gospel offers? Believe in a Person. "God so loved the world, that He gave His only begotten Son, that whoever believes in Him shall not perish, but have eternal life" (John 3:16). Do that, and your honest unbelief gives way to saving, life-changing faith.

Who Am I?

Jane Blasio's search for her birth parents led her to discover a dark secret. Soon the newspapers picked up the story, and the whole world knew.

In 1997, Blasio discovered that Dr. Thomas Hicks had arranged for as many as 200 illegal adoptions during the 1960's and earlier. Often, he led a birth mother to believe her baby died, then he sold the baby to families from a distant state. Blasio was one of those babies.

Paul Reymann saw the story and noticed some similarities. He, too, had been adopted. His birth certificate listed Hicks as attending physician. He learned that his parents had traveled out of state, paid the doctor in cash, and received him at the back door of the clinic.

Using DNA testing, Reymann located his birth father who welcomed a relationship with the son he never knew existed. Reymann said, "He could have just swept all of (his past) under the rug and I'd still be out there wondering. He is a man of great character, strong faith in the Lord and I just knew that everything was OK when I hugged him."

Blasio's and Reymann's converging stories have a common theme: the search for identity. That's not a quest unique to adopted people. "Who am I?" is the question we all ask in some way because it is connected to ultimate meaning. Today's world offers a menu of answers. Your identity can be sexual, political, occupational, or digital (social media). You can even take a personality test to "discover who you really are." These identities are incomplete at best, flawed at worst.

You will never know who you are meant to be if you remain alienated from your Creator. Jesus Christ came to fix that. You are created in the image of God, but the image is marred by sin, which separates you from God. By faith in Christ, you are re-created and restored. God has "reconciled us to Himself through Christ" (2 Cor. 5:18). The result is that sin no longer defines you. "Your body is a temple of the Holy Spirit. You are not your own. Therefore, glorify God in your body" (1 Cor. 6:19-20).

It is touching that Reymann found peace in the embrace of his birth father. How much more your Heavenly Father offers you a place in the family! "See how great a love the Father has bestowed on us, that we would be called children of God; and such we are" (1 Jn. 3:1).

As for Blasio, her birth mother died before they could meet. But that doesn't mean she doesn't know her identity. She writes, "If there's one thing in life I'm sure of...it's that God loves you and knows who you are and has known you from the beginning." She has found the answer to the question. Have you?

Reunited By Love

August 4, 2021

Guo Gangtang suffered a father's worst nightmare. In 1997, his 2-year-old son was abducted.

A 2015 movie, "Lost and Love," documents the Chinese man's epic search for his son. For two decades he traversed most of China handing out flyers and proclaiming his cause. He wore out 10 motorcycles while traveling some 300,000 miles. He slept under bridges, suffered bone crushing accidents, and endured highway robbery. But his search was unrelenting. He said, "Only by searching can I feel like a real father. It's impossible for me to stop." The movie ends as Guo continues in his cause, driven by love for his lost son.

Guo's persistence reminds me of Francis Thompson's poem, "The Hound of Heaven." These verses portray the relentless love of the Heavenly Father who pursues his children through the ups and downs of life.

Up vistaed hopes I sped;
And shot, precipitated,
Adown Titanic glooms of chasmed fears,
from those strong Feet that followed, followed after.
But with unhurrying chase,
and unperturbed pace,
deliberate speed, majestic instancy,
they beat..."

The poem's protagonist finally realizes what's happening and why. God seeks because He loves.

That is the message of Jesus' stories in Luke 15. The shepherd searched for one of his 100 sheep, then "calls together his friends and his neighbors saying to them, 'Rejoice with me, for I have found my sheep which was lost!' " The story of the woman rejoicing over finding her lost coin illustrates the "joy in the presence of the angels of God over one sinner who repents." But the story most like Guo's is about the father who ran to greet his lost son. The father says, "Let us eat and celebrate for this son of mine was dead and has come to life again; he was lost and has been found."

That hints at the rest of the story. This month, Guo and his wife found their lost son, now in his 20's. Seeing him, his mother cried, "My baby, you came back!" Their son's abductors had sold him in a neighboring province. He was raised well and had a university education. How must he have felt when he learned that his birth parents never gave him up for adoption, never stopped loving him, and never stopped searching for him! Guo reflected on the 24-year ordeal saying, "Everything can only be happy from now on!" The father's relentless search led to a joyful reunion.

Jesus's stories show that you, too, are the object of a great quest. Your story is God's story when by faith in Christ Jesus you are reconciled to Him. "He will exult over you with joy, He will be quiet in his love, He will rejoice over you with shouts of joy" (Zeph. 3:17). That is the Father rejoicing because you are united with Him by love.

Returning Word

August 11, 2021

"I am an attorney and would like to speak to you." Those can be ominous words, but it was actually a request for help.

Please allow a biographical note. I became a licensed civil engineer before I received a theological education. My engineering practice area is stormwater. So, I analyze and design bridges, roads, lakes, and drainage systems. I continued in practice until a few years ago when I accepted an instructor position.

The heart of stormwater engineering is understanding the part of the hydrologic cycle that predicts volume and rate of rainfall runoff. So, when the attorney called and said a business was suing the city over flooding, he wanted me to determine what happened and how to prevent it going forward. The hydrologic science tells the story.

Do science and theology mix? Of course! The Creator reveals much of Himself through the predictable order of nature. One of the world's greatest scientists admitted as much. Einstein said that the pursuit of science makes you aware of "a spirit vastly superior to that of man." He was amazed that mankind could describe the universe in mathematical formulas. Engineers rely on that predictability.

Science and theology mix when science is an apt metaphor for a spiritual truth. The hydrologic cycle is such a metaphor. "For as the rain and the snow come down from heaven, and do not return there without watering the earth and making it bear and sprout, and furnishing seed to the sower and bread to the eater, so will My word be which goes forth from My mouth. It will not return to Me empty without accomplishing what I desire" (Isa. 55:10-11).

What an image! God's word gives life, refreshes, and cleanses. It is predictable, visible, and constantly at work. And it produces what God desires. The power of God's word is evident because it brought the universe into being. "The worlds were prepared by the word of God" (Heb. 11:3). We know that Word to be a person, Jesus, through whom all things came into being (John 1:3).

What does God's Word accomplish? How does His Word not return to Him empty? The answer is in this: "I desire compassion, and not sacrifice, for I did not come to call the righteous, but sinners" (Matt. 9:13). God showers compassion on you by creating you and the world you live in. He has compassion by calling you to receive His great gift from the cross, forgiveness of sins. When you are reconciled to God by faith, the Word accomplishes what He desires. The cycle continues when others see the power of the Word in you.

God designed nature to be predictable and to reveal its Creator and His purposes. When the rain falls and the creek rises, it proclaims that God's Word does not return to Him void. Send it forth, Lord!

Real Faith

August 18, 2021

I attended a conference once, where one of the speakers mentioned the name Mo Anderson. A wave of admiration swept the cavernous hall. I didn't know her.

The folks at Keller Williams Realty do. In 1972, the former music teacher earned her real estate license. Two years later she set up her first office. In 1995 at the age of 57, she became CEO of Keller Williams Realty.

In her book, A Joy-Filled Life, she tells about a critical time in her faith journey. Her parents raised her in a Christian home, including church attendance, family devotions, and prayer. As a university student, a professor asked her class, "How many of you are Christians?" She raised her hand. "I'm here to challenge that," he said. After that, for five years she wandered in the wilderness of agnosticism, not sure if God exists or cares to be involved in her life.

When her son Rick was young, Anderson and her husband took him to Sunday School. They attended an adult class she considered boring. But one Sunday a bolt of lightning struck her thoughts: "Either Jesus was who He said He was, or He was the biggest liar and impostor the world has ever known."

The next day, she saw an ad in the newspaper. The local Lutheran church was advertising a basic class in Christianity, "Is Christ Real?" That is basic, because if Jesus never existed or isn't God the Son, and if his death and bodily resurrection didn't happen, then it is just religion, not Christianity. Anderson and her husband attended the class.

The first evening of the class, the pastor explained that the Bible is two books. "The first book, the Old Testament, is the history of a nation that gave birth to a man called Jesus. The second book, called the New Testament, is about this man's life and its meaning." Those words gave Anderson a framework for understanding salvation history, culminating in Jesus' death on the cross. She began to learn of the transcendent meaning of that event in terms of forgiveness of sin, new life in Christ, and the hope of eternity.

She had attended church for much of her life, but not until she was an adult did she place her faith in Christ Jesus as her Savior. She prayed, "I don't understand all of this, Lord, but I'm going to give you my life. I'm going to do my best, based on my understanding, to give you my commitment and my loyalty from this day forward." From that moment, her life has had purpose, direction, peace, and hope.

At that conference I mentioned, I had the opportunity to meet Mo. (She insisted I call her that!) I found her to be warm and engaging, and a woman of real faith. Is yours a story of real faith?

The Son of God has come, and has given us understanding so that we may know Him who is true; and we are in Him who is true, in His Son Jesus Christ (1 Jn. 5:20).

The Reconciliation

August 25, 2021

A walk-off, game-ending home run is not uncommon in professional baseball. But this was unique because it happened in an Iowa cornfield.

On Aug. 12, the Yankees and White Sox played the unique game near the movie set of "Field of Dreams" (1989). In the movie, Kevin Costner played farmer Ray Kinsella. Ray's father taught him to love the game. As a young man, Ray rebelled and became estranged from his father. After his father died, Ray hears a voice. "If you build it, he will come." He plows up corn to create a baseball field. Soon, ghosts of famous players appeared. After the last game as the ghost players disappear into the corn, the catcher removes his mask at home plate. It was Ray's father, who came to heal the pain of their separation.

The movie taps the human longing for reconciliation. We lament a broken relationship and wish it had not happened. We long for the way things were, for times of innocence. The best gifts from a parent are healthy childhood memories, our place of retreat - at least in our minds. Call it lived experience or hindsight, but we prefer calm over storms, simple over complicated, acceptance over rejection.

Living with past hurt is a Biblical theme. The beautiful city of Jerusalem, the center of life and worship, was desolate and ruined. The Babylonians sacked the city and deported the people. "In the days of her affliction and homelessness, Jerusalem remembers all her precious things that were from the days of old" (Lam. 1:7). But the people were not without hope. "The Lord's lovingkindnesses indeed never cease, for His compassions never fail. They are new every morning. Great is Your faithfulness" (Lam. 3:22-23). They had failed God, but He would not fail them.

Those who have experienced the kindness, forgiveness, and compassion of God have their deepest longings satisfied. "When the kindness of God our Savior and His love for mankind appeared, He saved us" (Tit. 3:4-5). When you round third base and look toward home you will see your longing realized. Your Heavenly Father awaits to reconcile with you, face to face.

Worldview Matters

September 1, 2021

Filmmaker Michael Moore weighed in on the Taliban takeover in Afghanistan. "They're religious nuts, but we've got those here too. Their Taliban, our Taliban, everybody's got a Taliban." His worldview sees no difference between Christians and Taliban.

The Taliban worldview and its interpretation of Sharia law has been on display for decades. Look no further than the attacks on 9/11. They believe their destiny is to rule the world, and to die in jihad is to enter paradise. This week, Afghans who enjoyed freedom, education, and opportunity are fleeing the Taliban. Many of them have become Christians and indicated as much on their national ID cards. Now those Christians, other "infidels," and anyone who resists the Taliban are marked targets and subject to atrocities.

Moore's own worldview would also rule the world. It denies God, so its moral foundation is the soft sand of individual preference. Reason is its authority, science is its sacrament, autonomy is its practice, and cancellation is its final judgment. To create its paradise, it targets and eliminates dissent. Its agenda of sexual liberation and expressive individualism creates its own victims. Moore's finger-pointing is ironic.

The Christian worldview explains the world as we experience it, i.e. the human sense of morality, the longings of the heart, the realization of beauty, the existence of evil, and the yearning for goodness and meaning. The concept that everyone has value regardless of their race, intelligence, gender, politics, wrongdoings, or health comes from Christianity. The Christian ideas of freedom, morality, and self-denial are the foundations of Western democracy. The historical resurrection of Jesus is the central proof of that worldview. As Paul explained to the sneering philosophers in Athens, God has "furnished proof to all men by raising (Jesus) from the dead" (Acts 17:31).

Speaking to people like Moore, who like the Taliban would cancel any public expression of Christianity, atheist Richard Dawkins said, "I have mixed feelings about the decline of Christianity, in so far as Christianity might be a bulwark against something worse." He's right. It is better to love your neighbor and your enemy, to be a good citizen and a servant to others. Christianity advances by love and inspiration. Logic would agree that the Taliban atrocities and progressive cancellation are something worse.

Moore's blind omission of the danger of his own worldview is predictable. But it is encouraging that many of the refugees from his worldview are finding liberation and healing by faith in the Lord Jesus and the truth He has revealed to us. I pray that the tragedy unfolding in Afghanistan causes America to rethink our drift away from the Christian worldview, which has contributed so much to human flourishing. We don't need more victims of bad ideas or refugees from a culture that has lost its moorings.

"He only is my rock and my salvation, my stronghold; I shall not be greatly shaken" (Psa. 62:2).

Your Ebenezer

September 8, 2021

God help us. That's a prayer, not a swear. How often those words escape our lips upon hearing news of Afghanistan, COVID, and American politics. You do remember He already has helped, right? You have to remember that to keep your sanity.

God's people wanted to remember. In ancient times, God gave them a victory. He sent thunder to confuse their enemy so they could reclaim their cities. Samuel set a symbolic stone near the scene of the victory and named it Ebenezer, which means "rock of help" (1 Sam. 7:12).

One evening when I lived in Haiti, I noticed the reflection of a significant fire nearby. I went outside and saw in the middle of the dirt road a fire consuming household items and various containers. A local voodoo practitioner was burning his occultic paraphernalia. In his advanced age, he embraced faith in Christ. The fire was his public recognition of God's help – his Ebenezer.

The U.S. has its Ebenezer, too. At 555 feet atop the Washington Monument, the highest structure in Washington D.C., an aluminum cap displays the words *Laus Deo*, meaning "praise be to God." In 1885, Americans reached to the heavens with this moving sentiment. It was their Ebenezer, and ours.

We have a rock of help that is more than symbolic. Jesus said, "I came that they may have life, and have it abundantly." He could promise that because as He said, "I and the Father are one" (John 10:10,30). Jesus shows you a reality that is beyond what you see, beyond what happens today, and beyond the bounds of time. He is your Rock of Help, now and forever. Your response, your Ebenezer, is to present yourself as a holy sacrifice (Rom. 12:1). The beautiful hymn lyrics say it well:

Here I raise my Ebenezer,
here by Thy great help I've come.
And I hope, by Thy good pleasure,
safely to arrive at home."

Whenever the news makes you want to utter, "God help us!" let it remind you that He already has. Raise your Ebenezer by presenting yourself to God as a living sacrifice, your greatest act of worship.

Season of Light

September 15, 2021

The nip in the air on Labor Day weekend signals a new football season. Hope springs eternal for sports fans. For some it's a fun game, but others look for a psychological boost from their team's wins. The new season is their window of hope.

This year, Tim Tebow had a shot at restarting his NFL career as a tight end for the Jacksonville Jaguars, but no. Tebow and Jaguars rookie quarterback Trevor Lawrence have both been outspoken about something unaffected by the football season - their faith. Lawrence said, "I put my identity in what Christ says, who He says I am."

I recently became aware that basketball standout Stephen Curry is also an outspoken Christian. Curry began his professional career in 2009. He has been named an NBA All-Star seven times and the league MVP, and has won three NBA championships. He said, "I think God has put me in this situation to change this perspective on what it is to be a man of God and a player in the NBA. I want to uplift His name. That's at the forefront of why I play the game."

What matters most to these men is not an athletic season but a lifetime of walking with the Lord. Because they responded in faith to the gospel of Christ, they see life in the light of God's sovereignty. That can work for you, too, as life comes at you in seasons. Your children leave childhood behind. You change jobs. Retirees contemplate what is next. Relationships change. Loved ones pass away. You have successes and failures. But these are only passing seasons.

Jesus said, "For a little while longer the Light is among you...While you have the Light, believe in the Light, so that you may become sons of Light" (John 12:35-36). He is that Light, and He invites you to embrace this as your season of response. To believe in Him is to join Tebow, Lawrence, and Curry as a son (or daughter) of Light. Seasons come and seasons go, but the season of Light is forever.

Not Going Away

September 22, 2021

I admire Peter Boghossian. The atheist professor refused to be muzzled. So, he resigned from Portland State University.

He couldn't continue teaching critical thinking and ethics due to university policies. He said, "Students are not being taught to think. Rather, they are being trained to mimic the moral certainty of ideologues. Faculty and administrators have abdicated the university's truth-seeking mission and instead drive intolerance of divergent beliefs and opinions." He called the school "a Social Justice factory whose only inputs were race, gender, and victimhood and whose only outputs were grievance and division."

Boghossian joins Christians in advocating for open inquiry. Censorship prevents strong arguments from seeing the light of day. It only countenances pre-determined conclusions, allowing weak evidence to be the only evidence. When people are denied access to robust dialogue about what's true and what matters, they parrot as their own the opinions of those who control the dialogue, all the while believing they are expressing an autonomous thought.

We are left with a culture that mocks the Creator's design for humans and the best expression of our humanity. That disordered view of reality creates victims. Christians engage our culture, but changing culture is not the end game. We want people to rise above the cultural confusion, to escape the cultural triviality and idiocy that leads to despair and hopelessness. Those victims need to hear the real story.

Christians tell the real story with scientific evidence that supports intelligent design. We appeal to the logic of objective moral values pointing to God. We share historical evidence that Jesus lived, died, and rose again. We engage our friends' opinions with honest questions. What do you mean? How do you know that is true? What difference does that make? What if you're wrong? The Truth will set you free!

Jesus engaged skeptics. He identified the problem - "Everyone who commits sin is the slave of sin," and offered the solution - "If the Son makes you free, you will be free indeed" (John 8:34-36). Even though people refused to believe Him, He lived, died, and rose again to make it real. Paul reasoned with thought leaders in the Areopagus. He mentioned "the times of ignorance," and the coming judgment. They sneered when he revealed that God raised Jesus from the dead. But Dionysius and Damaris heard the real story, and believed (Acts 17).

To follow the examples of Jesus and His servant Paul, we continue to engage the world we live in. We are called to such a time as this. With joy and hope, we beggars show other beggars where to find bread. Intolerance and cancel culture will not muzzle us. We love and associate with people who would shut our mouths. Our lives make the truth real, and we are not going away.

Finding Purpose

September 29, 2021

I thought Little Ricky on the "I Love Lucy" show was the real son of Lucille Ball and Desi Arnaz. Not true. His name is Keith Thibodeaux. Keith's life almost became a far worse Hollywood tragedy than a mistaken identity.

Arnaz selected him for the popular show in 1955 because he could play the drums. Later, he made appearances on "The Andy Griffith Show" as Opie's friend Johnny Paul. As he aged, Keith began to realize his good fortune. He asked his father, "Why did God pick me to do this?" His father answered, "God's got a purpose for you."

That line can a platitude, a throw-away response from someone who doesn't know what else to say. But that doesn't make it less true. That thought became a lifeline to Keith after his parents divorced due to his father's infidelity. He was angry at his father, show business, Hollywood, and ultimately at God. He turned to the party scene and the occult. He admits he began to hear tormenting, suicidal voices.

At the point of despair, Keith thought about God's purpose. He prayed, "If you're real, if you take me out of this mess I've made of my life, then I'll serve you." He attended a church service and had an intense experience. Sensing he was in the presence of Jesus, he felt unworthy because of his sinful lifestyle. He felt the Lord saying, "That's why I died." That day, he placed his faith in Jesus as his Savior. He said, "I had a whole new perspective on who Jesus is and what He did for me on the cross in dying for my sins, taking my sins."

At the time, he was the drummer for the rock band, David and the Giants. He shared his faith with them, and they also trusted Christ. In 1977, they became a Christian band. Keith married dancer Kathy Denton, and in 1986 they founded Ballet Magnificat!, a Christian outreach ministry. His search for purpose begun as a child bore fruit in his life as an adult.

What is your ultimate purpose? The Bible says you are "created in Christ Jesus for good works which God prepared beforehand." (Eph. 2:10). It says, "He who abides in me and I in him, he bears much fruit" (John 15:5). The Westminster Shorter Catechism teaches your purpose is "to glorify God and to enjoy Him forever." Taken together these mean you find fruitful purpose by abiding in Christ, which glorifies God and brings joy into your life.

Looking over his life Keith concludes, "God has used dance, he's used Ballet Magnificat, he's used David and the Giants to change people's lives, through what the Holy Spirit does through us. It's all about Jesus."

If "Little Ricky" can find purpose, so can you.

Fair and Just

October 6, 2021

I followed with great interest the plight of 15,000 Haitian migrants camped under a bridge in Del Rio, Texas. Living in their country for two years, I saw firsthand the wretched economic conditions and the desperation.

Illegal immigration is a political flashpoint, and I'll not take sides here. I don't have all the details, but the part of the story I find curious is that some Haitians were put on planes back to Haiti while others were put on buses to U.S. cities. Those deported must have felt it wasn't fair that the U.S. allowed the others to remain.

Years ago, a Haitian friend told me he had received a U.S. tourist visa. "Are you really just visiting," I challenged, "or do you plan to overstay your visa and get a job?" His answer was humbling. "Wouldn't you do anything you could to offer your children a better life? As an American, I don't think you could ever really understand." That made me realize that human ideas of justice will never be perfect, and we may never agree on what is fair.

The yearning for fairness and justice is hard-wired into our humanity. We yearn for wrong things to be set right. Yet even the justice of a holy God doesn't come across as fair to us imperfect humans. Is it fair that we are born into the human condition and inevitably fall under God's judgment? Are the murderer of children and the teller of

79

little white lies equally accountable to God? Is eternal punishment fair?

C. S. Lewis considers the objections to God's justice and writes, "What are you asking God to do? To wipe out their past sins and, at all cost, to give them a fresh start? But He has done so, on Calvary." So yes, we all commit crimes against God, and the impact of some are more horrendous than others. But the offer of forgiveness is the same. Jesus told of the vineyard owner who paid all workers the same though some worked less. The owner addressed the claims of injustice saying, "Is your eye envious because I am generous?" (Matt. 20).

Here is God's generous justice: "He Himself bore our sins in His body on the cross" (1 Pet. 2:24). Jesus' death procured perfect justice for us but it was not fair to Him. He was innocent of our ugly sin even as he made the cross beautiful to us. He made it possible for you to be declared blameless.

Those who would travel to the U.S. border seeking illegal entry do not know how laws will be enforced when they arrive. To immigrants and U.S. citizens alike, that is unfair and unjust. But if you want what is fair and just because it is offered equally and consistently to all, here it is: "Having been justified by faith, we have peace with God through our Lord Jesus Christ" (Rom. 5:1).

No Rewrite Needed

October 13, 2021

On the anniversary of Supreme Court Justice Ruth Bader Ginsberg's death, the ACLU tweeted a quote by her. The judge's 1993 statement was "dated," so the tweeter edited the engendered words and pronouns. A New York Times columnist complained, "It was somewhat Orwellian to rewrite historical narratives to suit modern sensibilities." One would think Ginsberg, the ACLU, and the NYT would be of the same mind. But times change; so do minds.

Much is Orwellian these days due to chronological snobbery, i.e. today's ideas are better than yesterday's. Christianity has not been immune to such "reinterpretation" (as though eternal truths change with the times). But let's not be "children, tossed here and there by waves and carried about by every wind of doctrine" (Eph. 4:14). We know that "Jesus Christ is the same yesterday and today and forever. Do not be carried away by varied and strange teachings" (Heb. 13:8-9).

We resist those waves and winds with a personal knowledge of God as Creator and Ruler of all. We know the creation did not create itself. God transcends creation and guides history toward the culmination of time.

Modern sensibilities hold that humans are basically good and simply need to tap our "better angels." The supposed solutions are self-help techniques and a cafeteria spirituality. This rewrite would deny that we are

81

marked by the dreadful stain of sin and separated from a holy God. In reality, we cannot hold any moral course on our own, which proves our brokenness. All have sinned, and we know it.

Another rewrite would make Jesus into a simple teacher of niceties whose death was an admirable example of dying for His beliefs. His Resurrection, of course, would only have been spiritual, certainly not physical and miraculous.

The real Jesus regarded Himself as God the Son, the Messiah, the object of your faith, the Savior of your soul. If this is not true, He was a false teacher. If true, His death and physical Resurrection change everything. Only Jesus bridges the vast gulf between you and the Father. This is not an exclusive claim because it is for all who believe.

We need absolute Truth, not a rewritten, updated religious tale. Professor Carl Trueman explains, "A gospel rooted in Scripture and based on the historical action of God in Christ is still the primary need of the world around us. Anything less is not just inadequate; it is in realty not historic, redemptive Christianity." The Scripture anticipates the allure of a form of godliness without power (2 Tim. 3:5). Any Orwellian rewrite of the loving, powerful, and true story of Jesus is a pitiful appeasement of modern sensibilities, a tossing by the waves and winds.

The older I am, the more I appreciate what stays the same. What God has said and done needs no rewrite because eternal truth stays the same, cultural waves and winds notwithstanding.

Searching for Eternity

October 20, 2021

Young people dream of being rich, and rich people dream of being young. That would explain why Amazon's Jeff Bezos and other billionaires are investing in startups like Altos Labs and Calico Labs.

These labs research how humans can live longer, even indefinitely. They focus on how to reprogram cells and turn back the biological clock. Scientist Shinya Yamanaka won a Nobel Price for discovering four proteins that reverse aging in cells. (Downside - they also cause huge tumors in lab mice.) Contemporary with this effort is the research of Israeli scientists who extended the life and health of lab mice with genetic modifications.

This pursuit of longevity is no stranger to history. The idea of cryonics, i.e., freezing the body in hopes of future resuscitation, has been around for 50 years. Eugenics and selective breeding were the predictable outcomes of Darwinism and contributed to 20th century horrors. Conquistador Ponce de Leon trekked through Florida looking for the Fountain of Youth. Indiana Jones searched for the Holy Grail...wait, that's fiction!

Anyway, here's what these folks are missing. Even if they were successful, they won't have the utopia they seek. Extended life would still suffer the ravages of the human condition. They will not eliminate sickness and injury, nor the mental anguish of fear, grief, and worry. Dishonesty, unfaithfulness, selfishness, and hate will remain. I'll give them this. They have the right idea, but they set their sights too low.

Our Creator hardwired the idea in us. "He has set eternity in their hearts" (Ecc. 3:11). So we search for the good that is beyond the ravages of time. C. S. Lewis wrote, "If we find ourselves with a desire that nothing in this world can satisfy, the most probable explanation is that we were made for another world. Earthly pleasures were never meant to satisfy it, but only to arouse it, to suggest the real thing."

How do we find the real thing? "God so loved the world, that He gave His only begotten Son, that whoever believes in Him shall not perish, but have eternal life" (John 3:16). Your search is over.

Give Credit

October 27, 2021

So, Captain Kirk made a trip to space! William Shatner struggled to express himself after his trip around the Earth in the Blue Origin rocket.

Moments after landing he told Jeff Bezos, "Unbelievable. The covering of blue...it's so thin, and you're through it in a moment. What you see down there is light. What you have given me is the most profound experience I can imagine. I am so filled with emotion about what just happened! I hope I never recover from this. It's so much larger than me and life. It has to do with the suddenness of life and death! OMG!"

I understand Shatner thanking Bezos, but he could have said more. If Shatner is still struggling for his lines, here's a cue: "When I consider Your heavens, the work of Your fingers..." (Psa. 8:3).

Consider a down-to-earth story. The widowed lady's grandson, Adam, lives hours away. She enjoys their fleeting moments together. His parents bring him to visit a few times each year. She decides to create a permanent reminder that she loves him, something that would be meaningful now and after he's grown up.

She begins to sort through her closets. She sets aside the cowboy-themed linens from his dad's childhood and shirts his grandfather wore. She finds the blue gingham dress she wore as a young mother, and the colorful, embroidered curtains from their first house. She still has some of Adam's baby clothes left behind from a visit a few years ago.

With material in hand, she begins the months-long task of making a full-size quilt. The arthritis in her hands and the fatigue in her eyes reduce the pace of the work but not her dedication to the task. When it is finished, she says, "It's beautiful, if I may say so myself. This is good."

She holds onto the treasured gift until Christmas. She wraps the box and marks "Adam" on the tag. "They will know it's from me," she muses. During their visit, the boy opens the box. "I've never seen anything like this!" he marvels, showing his parents. They are delighted with the colors, design, and usefulness of the quilt. But they never acknowledge she made the quilt. They do not recognize the sacrifice, creativity, and love that went into it. It never occurs to them to thank her. She loves them, nonetheless. I hope you see the parallel to Shatner's great omission.

You don't need a ten-minute trip in a Blue Origin rocket to be inspired to give credit where credit is due. "The heavens are telling of the glory of God; and their expanse is declaring the work of His hands" (Psa. 19:1). Consider the beauty and design of creation and worship the Creator! "Worthy are You...for You created all things" (Rev. 4:11). One day you'll see Him face to face and "O my God" will have new meaning.

Finding Happiness

November 3, 2021

British pop singer Adele says her latest album is for her nine-year-old son. She wants him to understand "who I am and why I voluntarily chose to dismantle his entire life in the pursuit of my own happiness." The three years making the album was a "self-reflection and then sort of self-redemption."

That's pitiful. No, it's tragic. She has internalized the pop psychology once expressed as "be true to yourself" and "follow your heart." Those are now the cultural doctrines and virtue signals of self-fulfillment, self-love, and psychological self-expression. But how is the pursuit of happiness virtuous when it requires someone else to lose theirs? Whatever happened to the virtue of self-sacrifice?

Jesus told us what it means to be a contented human being when he said the greatest commands are to love God and love your neighbor. In <u>Mere Christianity</u>, C. S. Lewis writes, "The happiness which God designs for His higher creatures is the happiness of being freely, voluntarily united to Him and to each other in an ecstasy of love and delight compared with which the most rapturous love between a man and a woman on this earth is mere milk and water."

God fashioned humans to find joy in relationship with Him and in imitation of His self-sacrifice. Yet humans think they can "invent some sort of happiness for themselves outside God," Lewis continues. "And out of that hopeless attempt has come nearly all that we call human history—money, poverty, ambition, war, prostitution, classes, empires, slavery—the long terrible story of man trying to find something other than God which will make him happy."

You need not spend years in self-reflection plotting your self-redemption. You'll not find what you seek rummaging through dusty bins in moldy corners seeking the treasure that could be yours by an outstretched faith and heavenward gaze. "Delight yourself in the Lord and He will give you the desires of your heart" (Psa. 37:4).

May the God of hope fill you (and Adele, her son, and his father) with all joy and peace in believing in Christ Jesus (Rom. 15:13).

Meta Verse

November 10, 2021

Mark Zuckerberg's new company name is Meta, meaning "beyond." He said, "The metaverse is the next frontier just like social networking was when we got started...A lot of us will be creating and inhabiting worlds that are just as detailed and convincing as this one, on a daily basis." Meta will reach beyond the Facebook brand and create a computer-generated reality. Wow, you can be an avatar!

Whistleblower Frances Haugen reports that Facebook knows but does nothing about the anxiety, depression, and suicidal thoughts caused by its social media products. What began as a clever way to share photos and news with family and friends has taken an algorithmic turn into psychology and manipulation. It replaces real human interaction with striving for "likes." In Screwtape Letters, C. S. Lewis wrote that it weakens a person to "abandon the people he really likes in favor of the 'best' people." He couldn't have known technology would invent a tool for that. What will stop the metaverse from weakening humanity further with its illusion of human progress?

Humans are gullible for illusions. You thought you controlled your Facebook feed but that was an illusion. Alec Baldwin shot and killed Halyna Hutchins – movie set safety was an illusion. A politician's call for a strong central government that guarantees safety, justice, and prosperity for all is an illusion. The greatest illusion is that you arrived in this universe by chance, and you are free to define your own meaning and reality.

G. K. Chesterton wrote, "The moment you step into the world of facts, you step into a world of limits. You may, if you like, free a tiger from his bars; but do not free him from his stripes. Do not free a camel of the burden of his hump: you may be freeing him from being a camel." Facts are part of human reality, and you cannot be liberated from them even if illusions, modern medicine, or technology tempt you to try. Here is a fact: you are created, and your reality is given to you, not created by you.

The word "meta" can also mean to be in association with someone. What if I told you about an association with Someone who can complete your reality with a love, joy, and peace that surpass all understanding? Here it is: "He rescued us from the domain of darkness and transferred us to the kingdom of His beloved Son, in whom we have redemption, the forgiveness of sins. He is the image of the invisible God...all things have been created through Him and for Him" (Col. 1:13-14,16).

That is a "meta verse" that is no illusion. It is reality. To associate with Christ by faith is to embrace reality and be truly human, just as your Creator intended.

He Is There

November 17, 2021

Winsome Sears immigrated to the United States from Jamaica when she was six years old. That was in 1963. Her name would not have been in the 2021 headlines except for her ability to survive a searing loss that few among us must endure.

When Sears was a child, her grandmother modeled a vibrant Christian faith, which Sears also embraced. When her grandmother died, Sears joined the Marines to learn discipline and leadership. After leaving the Marines, she and her husband moved to Virginia where she earned a college degree and became an elected official.

Sears left electoral politics to focus on her family. She and her husband started a small business, and she directed a homeless shelter. In 2009 she published a book about dealing with doubt titled, <u>Stop Being a Christian Wimp!</u> Two years later, tragedy struck. Her daughter and two granddaughters were killed in a car wreck. She recalls receiving the news at 3 a.m. "I just remember saying 'The Lord giveth and the Lord taketh. Blessed be the name of the Lord.'" I can't imagine the searing loss, the questions.

Professor John Lennox writes, "If Christian faith is worth considering, it needs to be deep enough to cope with our most heart-rending questions." When those questions erupt, it compounds the tragedy if you conclude that a good and loving God does not exist. The pain is real because evil is real, but God is present and has done something about it. The cross and resurrection of Christ Jesus are the divine intervention in human history to overcome the evil that besets us. Those events reveal an eternal reality beyond our present griefs.

God experienced the pain of grief. When his friend Lazarus succumbed to illness, Jesus wept after he told Martha, "Your brother will rise again" (John 11:23). They shared the pain of walking "through the valley of the shadow of death." But Jesus was there to embody the great promise, "I fear no evil for You are with me" (Psa. 23:4).

In God's Providence, good can come from pain. C. S. Lewis writes, "Pain insists upon being attended to. God whispers to us in our pleasures, speaks in our conscience, but shouts in our pains: it is His megaphone to rouse a deaf world." If tears help you hear from the One who promises a day of no more tears, then pain is redeemed (Rev. 21:4).

God values your life enough to make traveling this earth your opportunity to know Him. It helps that He chose to walk this path of pain Himself. He is a winsome God, and He invites you walk with Him in faith through your valley of the shadow of death.

Before her 2021 electoral victory Sears reflected on what her future might hold. Whatever it might be, she said, "You always know that God is there." The voice of experience.

Intentional Gratitude

November 24, 2021

If you could go back in time and thank someone, who would you thank and for what?

I posed that question in various forums. People named parents, grandparents, siblings, ministers, teachers, doctors, bosses, and neighbors. Some stepped in to raise children when the parents could not. Some loved by sharing time, truth, and help. People told of receiving unconditional love back when they were not very lovable.

I heard beautiful stories. Someone is thankful his grandfather as a young man had the audacity to interrupt a couple on a date in order to introduce himself to the young lady. The lady would become his grandmother! A WWII schoolgirl had a teacher who told her she was smart enough to continue her education. The now octogenarian lady is thankful that she is still learning. A next-door neighbor was a surrogate father to a boy whose single mom was raising six children. Many shared something like, "I would thank my grandmother because she introduced me to Jesus." That's the circles I run in, I'm proud to say.

That same Jesus encountered ten lepers who were keeping their social distance. He told them to go report to the authorities. As they did, they were healed. In their excitement, only one was intentional with his gratitude. He returned to Jesus, giving thanks and glory to God

(Luke 17). I wonder if the others remained ingrates. I don't want to be an ingrate.

So, I pondered how I would answer the question. My thoughts turned to 1969 when I was a boy, and our pastor came to our home. He explained about Jesus, what He did, and why it matters. For the first time I understood "whoever believes in Him shall not perish but have eternal life" (John 3:16). I should thank Pastor Webb, I thought. I searched for him online. Found his obituary.

The takeaways here are multiple. Express gratitude to whom it is due, while you can. It's always timely to place your faith in Jesus and to thank God. Sometimes in the exuberance of life you can forget to be thankful. It's good to be grateful for someone even if they're only a memory.

Please let me remind you to be intentional about thanksgiving. It's not just a day, it's a lifestyle. And there's something in it for you - gratitude is the fertilizer for the fruit of contentedness.

The 20th century poet Helen Steiner Rice penned this prayer about intentional gratitude:

O make us more aware, dear God,
    of little daily graces
That come to us with sweet surprise
    from never-dreamed-of places.
Help us to remember
    that the key to life and living
is to make each day a prayer of thanks
    and every day THANKSGIVING.

May you have reasons to be thankful and someone to thank.

Olasky's Story

December 1, 2021

Marvin Olasky is an academic, an author, and a Presbyterian. That's why it's an eyebrow-raiser when he tells about his solitary mystical experience.

In his book, <u>Lament for a Father</u>, Olasky explains he was an atheist (and Marxist) pursuing a PhD in American Culture in the 1970's. One afternoon he was reading Lenin. ("We must combat religion. It is the opium for the people.") He became distracted and fell into what he describes as a trancelike state. He sensed he was in a dark corridor with closed doors on both sides. He pushed one open and experienced an explosion of light. He knew it was God. For the next eight hours, he sat still while his mind raced with questions. Then he wandered the campus in the cold and darkness of night. The next morning, he was no longer an atheist.

One of his next steps was to read Matthew's gospel in Russian, focusing on each word. He read, "The Child who has been conceived in (Mary) is of the Holy Spirit. She will bear a Son; and you shall call His name Jesus, for He will save His people from their sins" (Matt. 1:20-21). He admits he did not want to be a Christian, but over the next three years he journeyed toward the truth about Jesus. He was a professor at San Diego State when he finally embraced faith in Jesus as his Savior.

Unlike Olasky, Richard Dawkins is still an atheist. But Dawkins likes Christmas traditions - singing carols, decorating a tree, giving gifts. He calls himself a "cultural Christian." That term could also apply to church attenders who reject the virgin birth and other miracles. If no supernatural or spiritual reality exists, then Jesus was only an attractive (and deceptive) religionist who impressed his followers so much that they thought they saw him alive after he died.

To reject miracles is to reject the Jesus of the Bible. Accept them and "you have a Savior who came voluntarily into this world for our salvation, suffered for our sins upon the cross, rose again from the dead by the power of God," writes Gresham Machen in <u>Christianity & Liberalism</u>. "The difference between those two views is the difference between two totally diverse religions."

Well-meaning people of an atheist or cultural religion mindset can enjoy the giving and good will of Christmas for now. Just be aware that the truth behind the trappings beckons you to consider who Jesus is, and to believe in Him as the living God, the God of miracles! Everything may look different tomorrow morning, per Olasky's own story.

The lyrics of the song "Jesus Saves," (Cottrell and Moffitt) include,

> *Day is breaking, night is quaking,*
> *God is making all things new. Jesus saves!*

That is Olasky's darkness-to-light story. "It's forty-five years later," he writes, "and my gratitude to God keeps growing. To God be the glory."

That can be your story, too.

Follow the Star

They missed the opportunity of a lifetime. A little curiosity would have led them to witness a miracle. Instead, they are characters in the Christmas story who are not part of a nativity scene. They didn't follow the star.

The magi from the east saw a star and followed it to Jerusalem (Matt. 2). They inquired about the birth of a king. Herod connected their request to prophecies about the coming Messiah. The scribes reported that 700 years prior, a prophet wrote that the Messiah would be born in Bethlehem (Mic. 5:2). So, the magi struck off toward Bethlehem. By themselves.

The scribes couldn't be bothered to find out for themselves if something wonderful was happening. Their prophet told of a "child born to us" whose name would be "Mighty God" (Isa. 9:6). The star signaled that defining event of all human history. The light beckoned their attention, but they met the moment with disinterest.

You make the same mistake if you ignore the light given to you. You see glimpses of light in classic Christmas movies. "It's A Wonderful Life" appeals to your yearning for goodness, selflessness, and love to prevail, and for greed, fear, and meaninglessness to be vanquished. In "White Christmas," you yearn for truth to overcome misunderstanding. The beauty, music, and warmth in the final scene with snow falling behind the Christmas tree is a contrast with the cold horror of war in the beginning scene. Why does the human heart yearn for beauty, goodness, love, acceptance, peace, and restoration? Those yearnings are the stars that lead the curious and guide the wise to truth.

In The Unknown God, Alister McGrath writes about these stirring spiritual yearnings. "In the end, only God can satisfy – precisely because we are made to relate to God, and luxuriate in His presence. Until we do so, our hearts will remain restless, and we must live with the pain of this desire and longing."

Your heart's deep yearning is your star, pointing you to the One who satisfies. Meet the moment and follow the star to the Light of mankind.

"In Him was life, and the life was the Light of men...There was the true light which, coming into the world, enlightens every man" (John 1:4,9).

She Knew!

December 15, 2021

In 1984, while developing a Christmas program for his church, Mark Lowery jotted down a poem. Seven years later Buddy Greene wrote a tune, and they recorded "Mary Did You Know" for the first time.

That poem emerged as Lowery pondered Mary's role in the historic moment that fulfilled prophecies and revealed mysteries. In a conversation with his mother (also a musician) she said, "If anyone knew for sure that Jesus was virgin born – Mary knew!" That led Lowery to jot down questions he'd like to ask Mary about what she knew. The popular song came from those questions.

Lowery emphasizes that the purely rhetorical questions are intended to express wonder and amazement, which are surely warranted. "I didn't mean to be profound, just pondering the mysteries of God Incarnate," he says, "of God with us, Immanuel! He had to become one of us to take away the sin of the world" (John 1:29). Lowery imagines exclaiming to Mary, "Can you believe who is in your lap!"

Lowery as a 26-year-old may not have meant to be profound, but the lyrics certainly are. They talk about the miracles of walking on water, healing the blind, calming the storm, and raising the dead. But those are not nearly as profound as "when you kiss your little baby, you kiss the face of God." Just who is this baby, this Jesus?

The lyrics unpack that question. "Your baby boy is Lord of all creation," who "would one day rule the nations." The final crescendo arrives with a question and an answer. "Did you know that your baby boy is Heaven's perfect Lamb? That sleeping child you're holding is the great I Am!" That is the very name of God claimed by Jesus Himself (John 8:58).

During his earthly ministry when Jesus spoke about entering the kingdom of God, his astonished disciples asked, "Who can be saved?" Jesus said, "With God all things are possible" (Matt. 19:26). That is what the angel Gabriel told Mary when he explained what was happening (Luke 1:37). That's all Mary needed to know.

That's what you need to know. All things are possible because God is with us!

Lifetime Joy

December 22, 2021

Perhaps your earliest recollection of Christmas joy is like mine. But the seedling thoughts of a child blossom into a mature, lifetime joy that survives what life brings - if you really get it.

When I was a child, Christmas was about lights and decorations, a break from school, visits to family, sweets to eat, and gifts on the big day. Those were only glimpses of joy. Charlie Brown's question was mine. "What is Christmas all about?" Linus offers the answer. "The angel said unto them, fear not. I bring you good tidings of great joy, which shall be to all people. For unto you is born this day in the city of David a Saviour, which is Christ the Lord" (Luke 2:10, KJV).

Childish thrills give way to this deep truth: those good tidings deliver a great joy to people desperate for it. The context of Christmas this year includes no-holds-barred politics, the latest variants of COVID, Chinese and Russian saber rattling, and inflationary pressures. On a personal level, someone in your life is hurting, and someone is gone. Can joy be found in the midst of desperation?

An ancient people were desperate, occupied by foreign powers for hundreds of years. Their prophets told of a coming Messiah, yet the world in solemn stillness lay waiting. Then Mary received a messenger saying she would bear the One the prophets foretold! She could not contain her joy! "My soul exalts the Lord, and my spirit has rejoiced in God my Savior. For the Mighty One has done great things for me and holy is His name" (Luke 1:46-47,49).

When Turkish author Senem Ekener lived in the U.S., Christmas time in the city and busy sidewalks dressed in holiday style were a new and joyful experience. But it was the story of Christ's birth that humbled her and led her to believe. "An indescribable amount of joy filled my heart and soul," she writes, "as I fully embraced the gift of salvation undeservedly given to me." She resonates with Mary's humility and the joy she found. "God incarnate revealed Himself to humankind through a young woman. This is my joy of the Lord." Joy is attractive, isn't it?

Jesus's intent is that "My joy may be in you, and that your joy may be made full" (John 15:11). God's grace expressed in the Savior is the gift of joy in a fallen world that offers no such gift. That's why we sing, "Joy to the world, the Lord is come!" Do you get it? That is no childish wonder or fleeting feeling. It is an abiding joy that is for a lifetime and eternity because it is the joy of the Lord. O come, all ye faithful, joyful and triumphant! Celebrate your Christmas joy!

Peace on Earth

December 29, 2021

I knew it was a risk. I meant it as an opportunity to express uplifting hope, and some saw it that way. Others didn't.

My social media question was, "What do you hope happens in 2022?" Responses included Jesus coming and COVID going. Some want peace for our sharply divided country. Others were content to bicker over politics and COVID mitigation measures, which illustrates why people want peace. I looked away for a minute and when I came back, the admin had mercifully disabled the commenting. I deleted the post. Sigh. "Can we all get along?" (Rodney King, 1992).

Among the many reasons America has no peace is this: we no longer have a common source for understanding what's real, right, and true. We live in an age characterized by, "Everyone did what was right in his own eyes" (Judg. 21:25). When a disillusioned country paints that picture long enough it looks like Haiti, which I've experienced. Division, corruption, hostages, violence, lawlessness. The beautiful, decent, God-fearing Haitian people don't want that for their country any more than we want it for ours. They need a peace their country cannot provide. So do we.

Jesus is the only hope for the abiding peace that you need. He warned of the ruler of the world coming, then promised to send His Spirit. "Peace I leave with you; My peace I give to you; not as the world gives do I give to you.

Do not let your heart be troubled, nor let it be fearful"
(John 14:27). That peace is His very presence with you.
That's how we survive this cultural moment.

One way to answer my social media question is the lyric
"Grown-up Christmas List" penned by Linda Thompson
and recorded by Amy Grant.

> *No more lives torn apart,*
> *that wars would never start,*
> *and time would heal all hearts.*
> *Everyone would have a friend*
> *and right would always win*
> *and love would never end.*

Of course, that won't happen until Jesus comes back,
but all is not lost. Trust the Prince of Peace and live by His
abiding presence. Then you'll have your own peace on
earth.

Disruptive Faith

January 5, 2022

The word "disruptive" comes to mind when I hear about someone who does not go along with the crowd. They stand out because they're different, hopefully in a good way.

I recently became aware of a certain University of Georgia professor, Henry Schaefer. He is the Graham Perdue Professor of Chemistry and Director of the Center for Computational Chemistry. He's a graduate of MIT and Stanford and is a pioneer in his field. He's also disruptive.

As an eager young professor in 1978, Schaefer's research demonstrated that a Nobel Prize-winning chemist was wrong about something. He has since published over one thousand scientific research papers. In 2004, scientists convened for a week-long conference in Korea to review and celebrate his work. He has directed over 100 doctoral students who are now professors all over the world. He is disruptive because his use of computers in chemistry caused scientists to think and research differently.

Schaefer is disruptive in another way. Many of his colleagues in the lofty airs of the academic community are proponents of scientific materialism (physical matter is all there is) and evolution (random mutations and natural selection explain life). He disagrees. In fact, he is an outspoken Christian. "There is no plausible scientific mechanism for the origin of life, i.e., the appearance of the

105

first self-replicating biochemical system," he says. "The staggeringly high information content of the simplest living thing is not readily explained by evolutionists."

Schaefer speaks around the world and explains his greatest discovery. "In 1973, I discovered the Jesus Christ of history, the Jesus whose life is described on the pages of the New Testament." He says, "I discovered that the resurrection of Jesus is not only historically true, but that it's one of the best-attested facts in all of ancient history." In 2003, he published his talks in a book, <u>Science and Christianity: Conflict or Coherence?</u>

Are science and faith in conflict? That's certainly what some would have you think. It matters because humans are born with ultimate questions of origin, meaning, morality, and destiny. To trust only science for answers is to make it something like a religion. The irony here is that modern science developed because early scientists assumed an intelligent creator. Science tells us the universe had a beginning and is fine-tuned for life. We know that cells contain genetic information to make life possible. All this is evidence for a creator who is apart from the material world.

That leads to the Jesus Dr. Schaefer discovered. "By Him all things were created, both in the heavens and on earth, visible and invisible...all things have been created through Him and for Him. He is before all things, and in Him all things hold together" (Col. 1:16-17). You have reasons to believe that, even if it's disruptive.

Religion or Relationship

January 12, 2022

I attended a conference where some highly respected people discussed and answered questions on a serious topic. Comedian Jeff Foxworthy was the moderator for the evening.

Foxworthy was so serious as he introduced the men sitting beside him as academics, intellectuals, and philosophers. Then he said, "Now let me explain what's happening here by borrowing from Sesame Street." Pause. "Remember that little song, 'One of These Things Is Not Like the Others'?"

That moment of self-deprecating humor opened the way for a lively discussion on reasons faith in Christ Jesus is rational and how the Biblical worldview uniquely aligns with how we experience the world. They (including Foxworthy) discussed meaning, suffering, and hope.

The Christian faith is "not like the others." I would summarize it like this: it is about relationship, not religion. For that formula to work, let me define religion as a moral framework for humans to overcome our flaws and a system to reach or satisfy a deity if it exists. Christianity explains that on our own, humans could never overcome our flaws and attain favor with God. Instead, God reaches for us and provides a relationship that mends the fallen human condition.

When God the Son became flesh and dwelt among us, He brought relationship. "Our Father," he taught us to pray. He referred to His followers as family (Luke 8:21). Friendship motivated His mission on earth. He said, "Greater love has no one than this, that one lay down his life for his friends" (John 15:13).

For years, Foxworthy has led a Bible study for homeless people at The Atlanta Mission. The fact that he shows up when he could be elsewhere offers its own lesson. It imitates how Jesus humbled himself and entered into human suffering so that he might offer you the gift of God, eternal life. It's the gift of presence.

Jesus lay down his life so you can have an eternal relationship with the Father and live a transformed life by the Spirit's presence within you. By faith you are a child of God (1 Jn. 3:1).

Faults and Forgiveness

January 19, 2022

Louisiana Gov. John Bel Edwards recently pardoned Homer Plessy. Plessy has been dead since 1925. What's this all about?

In the post-Civil War era, Plessy committed civil disobedience by violating a state law that required the separation of races in railroad cars. He appealed his case to the U.S. Supreme Court. In the Plessy v. Ferguson (1896) decision, the Court created the "separate but equal" doctrine. The lone dissent was Justice Harlan who wrote, "Our Constitution is color-blind and neither knows nor tolerates classes among citizens."

In the Brown v. Board of Education (1954) ruling, the Court began to fix its faulty reading of the U.S. Constitution. The Civil Rights Act (1964) further clarified constitutional freedoms. That history ultimately led to the descendants of Plessy and Harlan gathering with Gov. Edwards for a moment of repentance, forgiveness, and healing.

Another governor, George Wallace, stood in the way of freedom until an assassin's bullet paralyzed him. In 1979, he wheeled his chair into Martin Luther King, Jr.'s former church in Montgomery and admitted his faults. He said to them, "I can understand something of the pain black people have come to endure. I know I contributed to that pain, and I can only ask your forgiveness." They did. As MLK said years earlier, "Forgiveness does not mean ignoring what has been done...It means, rather, that the evil act no longer remains as a barrier to the relationship."

It takes courage to admit fault; it takes sacrifice to grant forgiveness. Courage, because humility is hard. Sacrifice, because you give up your right to retaliation. Repentance and forgiveness are part and parcel of the Christian experience because they express love for God and for one another.

Jesus told a story about a man who owed a great debt to the king. To settle the debt, the king planned to sell the man and his family as slaves. The man pled for leniency. The king felt compassion and forgave the entire debt. But the man went straight out and used harsh tactics to collect a small debt someone owed him. The king summoned the man and said, "Should you not also have had mercy on your fellow slave, in the same way that I had mercy on you?" (Matt. 18:21ff).

"To be a Christian means to forgive the inexcusable," wrote C. S. Lewis, "because God has forgiven the inexcusable in you." When you grasp how much you have been forgiven, you will be a forgiver. The Bible says, "Be kind to one another, tender-hearted, forgiving each other, just as God in Christ also has forgiven you" (Eph. 4:32).

The U.S. Supreme Court has more work to do in fixing its faults from the past. But whether it does or not, you have your own work to do. Be a forgiver, as you have been forgiven.

The Storied Life

January 26, 2022

Hiroo Onoda was a WWII Japanese army intelligence officer assigned to a clandestine operation in the Philippines. After the war ended, he refused to surrender for 29 years.

Onoda lived in a hut in the mountains, carrying out guerrilla activities. After the war, authorities dropped multiple leaflets with military information and family letters urging him to surrender. It was all propaganda to Onoda. He lived in ignorance of the truth that the war had ended, which prevented him from having a peaceful, civil life. After locating him in 1974, the Japanese government sent his former commanding officer to relieve him of duty. "Whatever happens," he had promised Onoda, "we'll come back for you." When he finally did, it meant Onoda was at a crossroad. He surrendered his sword. The Philippines later pardoned Onoda for crimes against their people. What a story!

Life is a story, isn't it? "Every man is hanging by a thread or clinging to a precipice," G.K. Chesterton writes. "Existence is a story, which may end up in any way." The rising action and uncertain information thicken the plot. The protagonist embraces the truth and resolves the conflict. The Japanese soldier might never end his war, but he finally did.

The Christian worldview sees a plot trajectory in all lives. In the rising action, the characters think they have sorted truth from propaganda. Yet, they live "in the futility of their mind, being darkened in their understanding, excluded from the life of God" (Eph. 4:17-18). But the truth leaflets keep dropping and finally someone comes and asks for their swords.

At that moment, the action stops. "All Christianity concentrates on the man at the crossroads," Chesterton writes. Will he see that the "truth is in Jesus" (Eph. 4:21)? The Lord Himself has come for him. "Yes, I surrender my sword!" he cries. By faith he accepts the truth and is included in the life of God. He is pardoned for his sin and prior disbelief.

How thrilling to see yourself in that story! It means "you lay aside the old self" and are "renewed in the spirit of your mind and put on the new self, which in the likeness of God has been created in righteousness and holiness of the truth" (Eph. 4:22-24). That renewal provides you the clarity to resist the propaganda of a culture that is untethered from reality and ultimate truth. You live a righteous and holy life because that's your new identity.

The life of faith is the denouement of the story, the new normal. It is the beginning of an amazing grace story, a story of love, peace, and purpose despite the daily reminders of your former clandestine life. You have a new story because something happened at that crossroads. You surrendered to the Truth. His name is Jesus.

Christian Courage

Christianity is for the courageous, even if you don't live in North Korea, China, or Afghanistan. Fear, worry, and despair common to the human existence call for the courage that is coincident with faith.

Persecution is real in North Korea. I read about a woman exiled to a life of hard labor because she is a Christian. She escaped to China. She collected food, medicine, and Bibles, and stole her way back into North Korea to meet the needs of fellow believers. Christian courage is evident in Afghanistan, too. There, church leaders changed their national identity cards to show they are Christians. Now the Taliban is hunting them down.

In the Open Doors USA 2022 World Watch report, Afghanistan tops the list for persecution of Christians. But China's communist party leads the way in using central control to punish Christians. Facial recognition, internet monitoring, and artificial intelligence are their tools to surveil Christians and create social credit scores. Low scores result in limited travel, employment, and education opportunities. Yet the church in China grows. More Chinese are Christians today than are members of the communist party.

Canadian authorities arrested and charged Pastor Artur Pawlowsky with multiple crimes for conducting church services in defiance of COVID restrictions. Californian John MacArthur did the same but wasn't arrested. Agree or not with their defiance, what they did took the courage of conviction.

It takes courage and sacrifice to be like Christ, to express the new life He has granted to you. Perhaps this is why the Father allows danger and trials to exist in the world. This is the proving ground of faith, the hardening of defenses against that adversary who "prowls around like a roaring lion, seeking someone to devour" (1 Pet. 5:8).

Courage energizes other qualities that characterize the Christian life. "Courage is not simply one of the virtues," C. S. Lewis wrote, "but the form of every virtue at the testing point...at the point of highest reality." Love, honesty, and humility shine the brightest, as does faith, when energized by courage. That's because they are such a contrast to the hate, deceit, and pride around you. "Prove yourselves to be blameless and innocent, children of God above reproach in the midst of a crooked and perverse generation, among whom you appear as lights in the world" (Phil. 2:15).

Regardless of who or what the opponent is, whether oppressive government, neighbor, co-worker, social media gadfly, or even your inner thoughts, God is not surprised and is equipping you for this moment. "Conduct yourselves in a manner worthy of the gospel of Christ...in no way alarmed by your opponents...For it is God who is at work in you, both to will and to work for His good pleasure" (Phil. 1:27,28, 2:13). Join the fellowship of believers worldwide who live unalarmed, above reproach, and with courage.

Who Are You?

February 9, 2022

His call surprised me, mainly because we were only somewhat acquainted. The pastor wanted me to speak at his church - Maranatha Baptist in Plains, Georgia.

Perhaps you associate the name of this church with peanut farming or the toothy grin of their famous Sunday School teacher. I accepted the invite, praying the Lord would speak truth, to me and to the church. Everyone wants to know truth, right?

On the appointed evening, I arrived early and took my place as the festivities began. A few minutes after the opening welcome, the farmer-teacher steps out of the evening darkness into the church, without wife or security shadow. He was one of four fellows the pastor called forward to take the evening collection.

Then I was up. The sermon text was Jesus' eyebrow-raising encounter at Jacob's well with a woman whose lengthy reputation followed her there (John 4). Yet He saw her. He knew her. He shocked her, not just by talking to her but asking for a drink. "If you knew who is speaking to you, you would have asked for water," He said. "He would give you living water." His well is different, far beyond what Jacob's well might offer.

He wasn't done with her. She wasn't done with Him either. She must have wondered, "Who are you?" He continued, "The water I give will become a well of water springing up to eternal life." Then He revealed just how much he knew about her, mentioning private details. That got her attention. She sought refuge from the probing conversation in her religious heritage, then spoke of the promised Messiah. That was his moment. "I who speak to you am He," Jesus said.

That's who He is. The promise fulfilled, the one who sees you, knows your name, and offers you the well of water springing up to eternal life. Jesus offers you a new identity in Him. By faith, that's who you are.

After the service in Plains, he was the first to thank me for the message. He said his name and shook my hand. "I know who you are, Mr. President," I said.

Intellectual Honesty

February 16, 2022

In his 1977 album, Billy Joel crooned about a love interest who was "always a woman to me." One of her endearing quirks was, "She never gives in, she just changes her mind!"

Politicians change their minds too. But lest you think poorly of them they say, "I misspoke," or, "My thinking has evolved." Translation: his staff told him the electoral winds are blowing in a different direction. Or in today's parlance, he didn't want to get canceled.

Of course, there are valid reasons to change your mind. When you think about thinking (metacognition) with an unbiased, honest attitude, you may well gain fresh perspective on truth. That's intellectual honesty. Dishonesty says, "My mind's made up. Don't confuse me with facts." That's also a version of confirmation bias.

Allan Sandage shocked the scientific community with his intellectual honesty. For background, in 1953 he earned a Ph.D. from Cal Tech in astronomy. As a prolific researcher and author, he won multiple science awards during his career. He was agnostic about God and embraced a materialistic philosophy.

In 1985, Sandage joined a panel of scientists at a conference in Dallas. The divided panel of theists and atheists were there to discuss the origins of the universe, complex life, and human consciousness. Sandage shocked his colleagues when he sat down with the theists. He had changed his mind. He explained that his research affirmed that the material universe had a definite beginning in time and space and had been finely tuned since the beginning to support life. That is clear evidence for a prior intelligence.

The Bible says, "By faith we understand that the worlds were prepared by the word of God, so that what is seen was not made out of things which are visible" (Heb. 11:3). Cosmology and astronomy gave Sandage reasons to believe this and become a Christ-follower. He said, "It was my science that drove me to the conclusion that the world is much more complicated than can be explained by science. It is only through the supernatural that I can understand the mystery of existence."

It is intellectual honesty to follow the evidence and change your mind. Sandage did.

Web Weaving

February 23, 2022

Willard Scott was the Today show weatherman until Al Roker succeeded him in 1995. His life calling was to bring joy to the world.

Scott started his career as a radio personality. His comedy show, Joy Boys, was popular in Washington D.C. When he returned to the show from his Navy stint, his new boss scheduled the show during the worst time slot. He applied this Biblical wisdom: "When someone wrongs you, it is a great virtue to ignore it." Despite the schedule, Joy Boys soon became the #1 show in that market.

Scott was the original Ronald McDonald and played Bozo the Clown. He brought his gimmicks with him to the Today show in 1980. He dressed as Cupid for Valentine's Day, wore a barrel on "tax day," and was a furry rodent for Groundhog Day. "People said I was a buffoon," Scott said. "Well, all my life I've been a buffoon. That's my act." His audience loved his act, especially his tradition of greeting centenarians on their birthdays.

But things weren't always rosy. Today Show host, Bryant Gumbel complained about Scott's "whims, wishes, birthdays, and bad taste." On his next on-air opportunity, Scott planted a kiss on Gumbel's cheek to show his forgiveness.

Scott was motivated by his Christian faith. He often said that if he hadn't become an entertainer, he would have been a preacher because he loved people. Early in his

Today Show career he said, "I am trying to weave a web of love. I want to make the whole country feel as if we are one. I may be a cornball, but I am me." He lived that out by forgiving people who hurt him, and by promoting joy.

What web are you weaving in your life? What is your unique purpose and style? Whatever your answer, let it be your expression of this highest calling: "I count all things to be loss in view of the surpassing value of knowing Christ Jesus my Lord" (Phil. 3:8).

In 2021, Scott flew away from the land of the dying to the land of the living. His web-weaving days are over.

Seeing Faith

March 2, 2022

In "The Last Crusade" movie, Indiana Jones pursues the holy grail. Near the end of the journey, he faces a chasm with no way to cross. "It's a leap of faith," he mutters, as he steps into the abyss. To his surprise, his foot lands on a bridge he cannot see.

On the other hand, it takes no climactic leap of faith for you to board an airliner to Paris. People have been riding the winds above the Atlantic Ocean for nearly 100 years since Charles Lindbergh showed us the way.

The difference between these two is blind faith vs. seeing faith. It matters because the Christian faith is not a blind faith. In its worst form, blind faith doesn't care about what is true – it believes anyway. Those who reject a religion of blind faith are right to do so, but don't accuse Christians of being taken captive by such "empty deception" (Col. 2:8). We see reasons to believe.

God has proven that He will reveal Himself in human history and reality. He showed Himself to Moses in the burning bush. Babylonian King Nebuchadnezzar saw a fourth person in the fiery furnace and was overwhelmed by the reality of God Almighty. Thomas doubted no longer when he saw and touched the resurrected Jesus. Jesus even showed his authority to forgive sins by making the paralyzed man get up and walk. All these encounters resulted in visible evidence – reasons to believe.

Do you see the evidence of the Bible itself? It had 40 human contributors spanning 1500 years writing in three languages, yet it is a coherent narrative of human history and experience. It has hundreds of prophecies, some very specific, all written centuries before Jesus fulfilled them. It explains what you see now: the universe exists, evil persists, and morality is universal. It explains why you yearn for beauty, admire innocence, and cling to life. It explains brokenness, justice, restoration, and hope. The Bible makes sense of the world as you experience it.

Do you see the evidence of creation? As you would expect, the more science discovers about the material world, the more it points to a prior intelligence. (I recommend Stephen Meyer's book, The Return of the God Hypothesis.) Creation is God's other "book." The Bible says, "His eternal power and divine nature have been clearly seen, being understood through what has been made" (Rom. 1:20).

Indiana Jones exercised blind faith in search of the cup that gives eternal life. That plot line appeals because eternity is set into the human heart (Ecc. 3:11). In the real world, to possess eternal life is to believe in a real Jesus who lived, died, and lives again. The evidence you can see is the foundation of your faith. Faith is not a blind leap into darkness, it's a step into the light.

War and Peace

March 9, 2022

Russia has invaded Ukraine. And we thought we lived in a world where blitzkrieg would never again change European boundaries.

Russian leaders ignore the message of a classic piece of their own literature. In <u>War and Peace</u>, Tolstoy weaves a tale of politics, patriotism, family, and the struggle of the human condition. In the end, the love and marriage of two young couples signal the hope of peace. The message lost on Russian leaders today is that peace is preferable.

The nations try but fail to achieve peace. After WWI, the feckless League of Nations watched WWII happen. In 1945 after WWII, the UN began. Think of all the world peace since then! The permanent members of the Security Council cannot even bring themselves to be peaceful. Russia and Ukraine currently serve together on the UN Human Rights Council, but did that stop the clanking war machines?

So how shall we think about these things? Here is a framework for thinking from a Biblical worldview.

(1) We will always have wars and rumors of wars until the day Jesus returns. Wars are a reminder that this is a fallen, temporary world. "See that you are not frightened," He said, "for those things must take place" (Matt. 24:6).

(2) That day may be immanent. Or not. If the Lord tarries, it's for the purposes of grace and salvation for those who believe. "The Lord is patient toward you, not

wishing for any to perish but for all to come to repentance" (2 Pet. 3:9).

(3) We can work for peace on earth, but making a warless world is not the Christian's ultimate objective. We have a higher commission, to rescue victims from the chaos of separation from God. To be reconciled to God is to be a follower of Jesus. He said, "Make disciples of all the nations...teaching them to observe all that I commanded you" (Matt. 28:19-20).

Join me in praying for the Ukrainian people bloodied by the claw of the Russian bear, and for those hapless Russian conscripts taken from their mothers. Pray "deliver us from evil," that people and nations would know the peace of Christ.

Enduring Insults

March 16, 2022

The 2022 MLB season is delayed by an owner-initiated lockout that ended after 99 days. After two years of pandemic, baseball fans just want it to be about the game. When players started anthem-kneeling in 2017 and Commissioner Manfred moved the All-Star game in 2021, fans longed for simpler times.

Those simpler times may exist only in your memories of little league or neighborhood sand lot action. Even back in 1945, times were not simple. That's when an honorably discharged U.S. Army veteran signed to play for Branch Rickey, manager of the Brooklyn Dodgers. Rickey was an innovator. He introduced the batting helmet, pitching machines, and the farm system. He also introduced the world to his new recruit, Jackie Robinson.

Rickey and Robinson's meeting at Dodgers headquarters had the makings of a historic moment, not just for baseball. Robinson would be the first black player in the league. "I know you're a good ballplayer," Rickey said. "What I don't know is whether you have the guts." Rickey wasn't talking about Robinson staring down heaters in the big leagues but facing the threats to his life and attacks on his dignity. "I'm looking for a ballplayer," Rickey said, "with guts enough not to fight back."

Knowing it would not be easy or simple, Rickey shared with Robinson the words of Jesus. "I say to you, do not resist an evil person; but whoever slaps you on your right cheek, turn the other to him also" (Matt. 5:38). By this Jesus put personal retribution and revenge out of bounds. Jesus knew about emotional intelligence, self-awareness, and self-management before Daniel Goleman popularized the terms. It matters because to lose control is to lose sight of your mission. When we who share the life of Christ are wronged, that becomes our opportunity to sacrifice our egos, serve others, and love our neighbor.

Robinson accepted the charge from fellow Christian Rickey and history celebrates Robinson's story. Eric Metaxas writes about Robinson, "With God's help, one man lifted up a whole people and pulled a whole nation into the future." All because a man of faith simply applied the words of Jesus to turn the other cheek.

Faithful in Prayer

March 23, 2022

*The effective prayer of a righteous man
can accomplish much. (Jas. 5:16)*

War is horrible. What's happening in Ukraine is no different. We have the technology to watch it unfolding in real time. That gives the illusion that we know everything that's happening and why. We can know this: laying siege to cities, killing people, and destroying property are evil.

War doesn't change. Ancient history records Assyrian King Sennacherib invading the land of Judah. His tactics were like Russia's only without tanks, jets, and missiles. At one point, he sent a letter calling for surrender by Judean King Hezekiah. Hezekiah's response was to remain faithful to God.

His response is worth considering as you pray for Ukraine and as you face your own personal trials. Hezekiah's prayer (2 Ki. 19:14-19) reveals the heart of a faithful believer.

(1) Hezekiah "spread it out before the Lord." He acknowledged the problem was beyond his control and took it to the Lord as an act of worship.

(2) "You are the God of all the kingdoms of the earth." There is no place on earth that is beyond God's reach or view. He has the power to intervene. He is Sovereign.

(3) "The kings of Assyria have devastated the nations." It helps to name the specific dangers that concern you. Take the facts of the situation to God in prayer.

(4) "Deliver us from his hand." Likewise, Jesus taught us to pray that the Father "deliver us from evil." We know what evil is because we have a moral law embedded within us by a moral Lawgiver. But evil does not have the final say. "God causes all things to work together for good to those who love God" (Rom. 8:28).

(5) "That all may know that You are God." May God make Himself known to a doubting world, may His will be done, and may he be glorified in your situation and your reaction to it.

This is not a formula to persuade God to fix everything that's wrong, like forcing Russia to retreat from Ukraine. (To be sure, THAT would be a miracle). Rather, this is the posture of a believer who acknowledges the hand of Providence in human affairs. The believer who trusts that God will accomplish His purposes in the world is the believer who is faithful in prayer.

Restless Heart

March 30, 2022

Some years ago, our county installed a kayak launch in a park on the headwaters of TVA Lake Nottely. I decided to enjoy the amenity in a different way than other boaters.

I grew up in the country close to a river. Summer days fishing in the creek (only after doing my chores), camping under the stars near the swamp...I was Tom Sawyer and Huck Finn. Maybe a return to childhood is why I launched my skiff in the Nottely at dusk. I drifted downstream. The kayakers were gone but I was not alone. I lit my lantern as the orange glow sank into the western sky.

It was as though nature began turning up the volume. Peepers, bullfrogs, crickets, and other noisy insects competed for airtime. A screech owl and a lone whip-poor-will added to the chorus. Against the moonlit sky, bats darted about for supper. My presence convinced something heavy to splash nearby. I was mesmerized. I captured audio to share online, but I couldn't capture the moment.

Recently, I came across the work of Gordon Hempton, a professional sound recorder. He struggled to describe the Amazon rainforest at dusk. "I begin to hear the insect patterns, and how each rhythm is a different insect, especially as the light weakens," he said. "Oh my God! I realized this is the sound of the spinning Earth, like a huge clock. It's just so elaborate and precise, beyond human invention." He was mesmerized, too.

Cut to images of destruction and death in Ukraine. Mothers crying. Refugees attacked. Conscripts captured. Body bags. Smoke. Fire. Pleas for help.

The contrast is wrenching. The peaceful chorus of nature at dusk vs. the agonizing cries of humans at war. It points to the deep longings of a restless heart. God reveals much about us through contrasts, which draw out those longings. We desire peace, not war; love, not hate; safety, not danger. We admire wisdom, not ignorance; beauty, not ugliness; sacrifice, not selfishness. We cherish life, not death.

The contrasts stir your restless heart for answers. Here is one. "He is not far from each one of us; for in Him we live and move and exist" (Acts 17:27-28). In Jesus, your soul has peace, love, safety, and wisdom. He sacrificed His life and makes beauty from ugly so you may enjoy a fulfilled life even when wrong seems strong. The hymnist mused about the music of the spheres, the birds their carols raise, and hearing Him pass in the rustling grass. Then this:

Oh, let me ne'er forget,
   that though the wrong
   seems oft so strong,
God is the ruler yet.
This is my Father's world.

The sublime and suffering on earth point your heart heavenward to find peace and meaning. "Thou hast made us for Thyself," Saint Augustine wrote, "and our hearts are restless until they find their rest in Thee."

Mystery Revealed

April 6, 2022

If you like mystery shows, the "Poirot" TV series based on Agatha Christie's novels is probably on your radar. British actor David Suchet played the title role from 1989 to 2013. During that time, he was trying to solve his own mystery.

In his book, <u>Behind the Lens,</u> Suchet tells his story. He was enjoying his career as a successful actor. In 1986, he traveled to America. In his hotel room soaking in a hot bath, his thoughts randomly settled on the afterlife and resurrection. That surprised him because until then he had been agnostic about such things.

He decided to read the Bible. Not knowing where to begin and having some historical interest in the Roman Empire, he began in the letter to the Romans. Its probing truths attracted him. "If God is for us," it says, "who is against us? Who will separate us from the love of Christ?" (Rom. 8:31, 35). "I came across a passage," Suchet said, "that spoke of a way of life I wanted to be part of...a coherent philosophy I could really relate to. Christianity offered me that. The Christian worldview is love."

That hot bath in 1986 began Suchet's journey as a reluctant convert. He wasn't sure what to make of the resurrection of Christ. In 2007 after years of analysis, he found the evidence for the resurrection plausible and the way of faith veritable. Mystery solved. He believed in Jesus Christ as revealed in the Bible.

Suchet is right to consider the physical, attested, bodily resurrection of Christ as central to the Christian faith. "The whole of Christianity is based not only on the death, the crucifixion, of Jesus, but also on the resurrection," he says. "The early Christians believed He was divine because of the resurrection and without the resurrection, there is no faith. You cannot separate the cross from the resurrection, which is the greatest miracle justifying Christian belief in Jesus' divinity." That's a good paraphrase of 1 Cor. 15.

The Bible connects Christ's love and resurrection. "Christ Jesus is He who died, yes, rather who was raised, who is at the right hand of God, who also intercedes for us." In a grand crescendo it declares that nothing, not even death, can separate us from the love of God which is in Christ Jesus our Lord (Rom. 8:34-39). In love Jesus died as a divine sacrifice for your sin, and in love He arose from the dead as evidence of your eternal life. Jesus' love for you is displayed in history and is no mystery.

Suchet has pursued his new passion by making documentaries about Paul and Peter, and by audio recording the entire Bible. He wants to make it known that Jesus is the Christ, the mystery revealed. Your response? Believe and rejoice!

Doubt to Belief

April 13, 2022

If you ever doubted the resurrection of Jesus Christ, that's understandable. The central feature of the gospel is also the most challenging. In fact, Thomas followed Jesus for years and heard Him explain the resurrection, yet Thomas couldn't get his head around it.

When his friends said, "We have seen the Lord!" Thomas didn't say, "Sure, Jesus will always be alive in our hearts because we remember him fondly." He didn't assume they were hallucinating in their collective distress or were describing a "spiritual" resurrection. No, he heard them speaking of a physical resurrection and he demanded evidence. "Unless I see in His hands the imprint of the nails...and put my hand into His side," he said, "I will not believe."

Jesus heard him and waited eight days. Then it was Thomas' moment. Jesus appeared and told him, "Reach here your hand and put it into My side, and do not be unbelieving." He invited Thomas to see and touch His physical body. Overwhelmed Thomas exclaimed, "My Lord and my God!" (John 20:24-28).

Today, doubters deny the physical resurrection by appealing to science and naturalism, and thereby dismiss the entire gospel of Christ. Medical science says no mechanism exists by which someone dead for three days can live again. Naturalism says the material world is all there is. That *a priori* assumption hasn't worked.

Scientists have yet to advance a naturalistic hypothesis about the origin of the universe that they can prove.

But to the point, "Christians do not claim that Jesus rose by some natural mechanism," John Lennox writes. "They claim that God raised him from the dead. And if there is a God, why should that be judged impossible?" The God who creates also resurrects.

The physical resurrection of Jesus Christ matters. "If it is true, it is the supreme fact of history," Norman Anderson writes, "and to fail to adjust one's life to its implications means irreparable loss." This can be your moment to adjust from doubt to belief. As Jesus told Thomas, "Blessed are they who did not see, and yet believed" (John 20:29). Was He talking about you?

He Is Risen!

Love vs. Power

April 20, 2022

The whole incident started during the pre-dawn hours in a village in Haiti where I lived. I was shocked at how attractive the lie was.

My job included making the daylong journey to Port-au-Prince to purchase supplies. It was a cash economy, so I had $400 in my backpack. I left in the wee hours of a moonless morning. The absence of electricity and the inky darkness masked whatever lurked about.

I drove the Land Rover to pick up a companion. I stopped beside his house and walked a few steps to his front door. Was that a noise behind me? I looked into the darkness. Nothing. As we climbed in for the grueling trip ahead of us, I checked the back seat. My backpack was gone, along with the money. So were my plans for the day.

I learned later that a healthy young man had followed me, hoping to hitch a ride to the city. Seeing my backpack, he couldn't resist the crime of opportunity. He had never seen that much cash. The next day, he checked himself into the hospital. A few days later...he died. The Harvard-trained doctor who attended him told me he died from shock and fear. Seriously.

As I tried to get my head around that, Renoll from the village came to see me. I suspected Renoll of petty theft, but never accused him. He said, "Now everybody knows you have power." Then he pleaded, "You know I never stole from you, right?" For a moment, I marveled at my newfound "power." The voodoo culture would expect me to exploit it. Then it hit me. To embrace that attractive lie would change my mission from love and truth to power and deception. I told Renoll that I forgave the thief, because God forgave me through Jesus' death on the cross.

The voodoo culture has something in common with our popular culture. They both pursue and abuse power as the supreme goal of human existence. In this cultural moment, history, identity, reality, and language all depend on who's in power. What a contrast with the Christian worldview of loving God and neighbor by believing and offering truth!

Love does not abuse power or endorse lies. It "rejoices with the truth" (1 Cor. 13:6). Jesus promises power "when the Holy Spirit has come upon you; and you shall be My witnesses" (Acts 1:8). His power is not for personal gain but for truth-telling. The Christian's calling does not align with a power culture's denial of the obvious and attempts at mass deception. Now is our time to refuse to repeat the lies and speak the truth boldly and kindly, whatever the consequences. When you do, "It is not you who speak, but it is the Spirit of your Father who speaks in you" (Matt. 10:20).

I regret the death of the young man. If I had gone to his bedside and offered forgiveness, love might have set him free from the cultural lie that allowed fear to destroy him.

Receive a Child

April 27, 2022

I shudder to think about what's happening to children at the hand of adults these days. It's not the world I grew up in. Maybe every generation says that...

My parents raised me in a community that cared about children and respected a parent's responsibility to raise them well. My parents were not the only adults who were formative in my life. Others received me into their sphere of influence and invested in my growth and development.

The public school I attended hosted the traditional first grade play. From among the 40 or so first graders, one would recite the 23rd Psalm and lead the Lord's Prayer. Our teacher Lila McDuffie selected me and helped me prepare. I was confident as I stepped behind the "pulpit" and faced the audience.

Before young Gloria Thurmond (see autobiography Gloria!) set out on a lifetime of missionary service in Bangladesh, she visited my church's Sunbeam class for children. She appeared wearing a traditional sari, a long cloth garment that could be worn in various ways. Suddenly, the world seemed smaller and less mysterious to me, with fascinating cultures different than the deep South.

Edgar Davis was a pastor to our community. When I was 14, he asked me to play hymns on the piano for the worship service he conducted at the nursing home. Walking those halls my young eyes saw shocking things, but he talked me through it. He helped me see that ministry includes serving people outside the walls of a church building.

Don Tennyson formed a contemporary Christian youth band and ensemble when I was 16. He selected me for the band. It was a heady experience when we procured a touring bus and took our troupe on the road for 10 days. What started out as fun turned into hard work, problem solving, and relationship management. We grew up a lot on that trip.

Here's your takeaway. Invest in children. Let them see your faith in action. Train them by providing opportunities to serve. Protect them from "the serpent of old…who deceives the whole world" (Rev. 12:9).

Children matter to God. "Whoever receives one such child in My name receives Me," Jesus said. "But whoever causes one of these little ones who believe in Me to stumble, it would be better for him to have a heavy millstone hung around his neck, and to be drowned in the depth of the sea" (Matt. 18:5-6).

While the millstone factory is working overtime for those who confuse children about gender and sexuality, you have a better option. Receive a child. Train him in the way he should go. Give her hope and opportunity. And some day a man like me will reflect on his life and remember that you did, and he'll credit you with why he did the same.

A Woman's Value

May 4, 2022

William Shatner, Paris Hilton, and other celebs are buying and selling NFTs. I had to look up NFT – "non-fungible token." I still don't understand what they are, so they clearly have no value to me.

To value something, you must first know what it is. Take women for example. In a bizarre cultural twist, we have forgotten what a woman is. In her Senate confirmation hearing, Ketanji Brown Jackson gave voice to that amnesia. Sen. Blackburn asked her to define the word "woman." "No, I can't," Jackson said. "I'm not a biologist." By denying what has been obvious and understood since the beginning of history, the culture devalues women.

Jesus never devalued women, but the Roman and Jewish cultures of the first century did. Women had lesser legal status, and men treated them as possessions. That's one reason Jesus was a revolutionary figure. He scandalized the powers that be by respecting, affirming, and teaching women. God the Son created male and female in His own image, and He values both.

Jesus encountered a woman at the Sychar town well. He was alone with her, spoke to her, and asked to drink from her container. His disciples were shocked when they returned to find Him in a theological, intellectually challenging dialogue with her. And for the first time, He revealed that He is the long-expected Messiah. To a woman! (John 4)

The historical record indicates that women were witnesses to the greatest news the world has ever known. Mary Magdalene, another Mary, and Salome witnessed His death and resurrection (Mark 15-16). In fact, all four gospels record women visiting the empty tomb of Jesus. God inspired the gospel writers to record these women's witness to these events.

If you want to know who you are as a woman, go to the One who created, loves, and knows you. In Him, you will find your value and identity.

I know what a woman is. I value the women in my life, starting with my wife and mother. As for an NFT, well, it's a "unique crypto token managed on the blockchain." It's valuable, especially to whoever created it and knows what that is.

First Freedom

May 11, 2022

The U.S. Supreme Court continues to wrestle with religious freedom. That's no surprise, given the secular trajectory of American culture.

The latest case involves Joe Kennedy, a high school coach in Bremerton, WA. His practice of praying on the field after football games cost him his job. Previous religious freedom cases include Jack Phillips from Lakewood, CO and Baronelle Stutzman from Richland, WA. They both faced civil penalties for refusing to violate their deeply held religious beliefs in the conduct of their businesses.

Religious freedom is the first freedom in the Bill of Rights. The founders believed Congress should neither establish a state religion nor prevent citizens from practicing their faith. On this principle the other freedoms stand. It's the bellwether freedom, the "canary in the coalmine." If America cannot find the fortitude to protect this freedom, the others are in jeopardy as well.

Religious freedom is for everyone and is rooted in the Christian worldview. In his book, <u>Liberty in the Things of God</u>, Robert Wilken points to three supporting Biblical themes. (1) Faith is accountable only to God and cannot be compelled. (2) Faith carries an obligation to act. (3) Human affairs are governed by both God and the state. These themes call for religious freedom and are worth a closer look.

Jesus doesn't compel. He invites. "Come to Me, all who are weary and heavy-laden, and I will give you rest" (Matt. 11:28). If religion is coerced, it's not authentic. God knows if faith is authentic. "No creature is hidden from His sight" (Heb. 4:13). You are accountable to God for what you believe, not to government or cultural watchdogs.

Beware the term "freedom to worship," a stealthy redefinition of religious freedom. It limits acts of faith to private practice or a house of worship. The Christian faith is personal but not private. It is an obligation to act in public. "Faith, if it has no works, is dead (Jas. 2:17). When the authorities tried to compel the disciples to change their public actions, Peter replied, "We must obey God rather than men" (Acts 5:29).

God grants government the authority to keep public order (Rom. 13:1-7). Jesus acknowledged government's role when He said, "Render to Caesar the things that are Caesar's; and to God the things that are God's" (Matt. 22:21). God's ideal is for you to be a faithful believer and a good citizen of a country that restrains evil. Faith and government can coexist. Religious freedom is good government. I pray the U.S. Supreme Court knows that.

To make this personal, the erosion of religious freedom cannot prevent you from believing (e.g., Christians in China, Iran, North Korea). The good news is that you have every reason to place your faith in Christ Jesus, receiving the forgiveness, peace, and hope that He gives. Faith in Christ means freedom from the penalty of sin. To believers, that is our first freedom.

Forgiven and Reconciled

May 18, 2022

Vox.com recently published articles on "America's struggle for forgiveness." From what I read, Vox should have talked to some regular Americans before posting.

Vox writer Sean Illing offers his diagnosis of the problem. "A lot of people, with good reasons, point to social media and 'cancel culture' as evidence that we're becoming a more punitive society. I do think that the internet has made us less forgiving, and I worry that the world we've built has supercharged our worst pathologies." In the article, he hardly masks his bias that people who do not share his moral high ground have more pathologies to forgive.

Aja Romano maps out the hopeful stages of resolving toxic disagreements. "What we would hope to find after that initial period of outrage is discussion, apology, atonement, and forgiveness." But that's not happening per Atlantic writer Elizabeth Bruenig. "As a society we have absolutely no coherent story — none whatsoever — about how a person who's done wrong can atone, make amends, and retain some continuity between their life/identity before and after the mistake."

Isn't it interesting that religious language finds its way into the discourse? These writers miss the point that theologians have known all along. Everybody needs forgiveness. None of us occupy the moral high ground and all of us share the worst pathology – the fallen human condition. And Jesus does offer a coherent story about forgiveness and reconciliation.

It matters because forgiveness is a quality-of-life issue. It's also a faith issue. Jesus draws a direct link between those who forgive and those who are forgiven. He wants you to offer others what He offers you. "If you forgive others for their transgressions," He said, "your heavenly Father will also forgive you" (Matt. 6:14). When you understand the depth of your depravity and how much God forgives you, you become a forgiver. You leave the offender in God's hands. It is liberating to release that pathological drive to control others and sustain outrage. Faith, love, and forgiveness make a high-quality life.

Linda Bagley has that kind of life. In court, she had something to say to James McCleary. His impaired driving killed her son and daughter-in-law. She forgave him. Her daughter added, "Mr. McCleary, make your life right with God because that's who we all answer to in the end." Afterwards, Bagley gave McCleary a lengthy, tearful embrace. Her faith empowered her act of forgiveness and reconciliation.

C. S. Lewis suggested it is easier to forgive the single great injury than the incessant provocations of daily life, "the bossy mother-in-law, the bullying husband, the nagging wife, the selfish daughter, the deceitful son – how do we do it? By remembering where we stand." By faith in the Lord Jesus, you stand forgiven and reconciled to Him. That's the reason to forgive, something Vox could learn by interviewing forgiven people.

A Blessed Day

May 25, 2022

Dear young lady at the front desk, I wish we'd had more time to talk.

You probably tell all the guests, "Have a blessed day!" as they leave. I'm the guy who asked, "What do you mean by blessed?" I wondered about your beliefs. "Just that good things happen for you today," you said. I followed up, "And where do blessings come from?" It was early in the morning, and you caught me off guard. "From the universe, right?" What a great conversation starter, if it really was a question. Here are a few thoughts to ponder.

For the universe to give a blessing, it must be able to think and act benevolently. Since the universe is material, does that mean the rocks of planets, burning gasses of stars, and gravitational forces in galaxies form a sentient being? Seems far-fetched.

Let's talk about the universe. Since it had a beginning, wouldn't that suggest something or Someone caused it? Such a first cause would logically have to be outside of the universe since nothing causes itself. Wouldn't the Someone who caused a universe of beauty and order and gave you life be a more likely source of blessing?

You defined blessing as "good things." Where does your sense of good and evil come from? Could a material world that just "is" produce beings that have a sense of what "ought" to be? Yet we do have a sense of what is good, righteous, and just. In his early life, the WWI veteran C. S.

145

Lewis doubted the existence of God because the world is so evil and unjust. "But how had I got this idea of just and unjust?" he wrote. "A man does not call a line crooked unless he has some idea of a straight line." Lewis concluded that God created us with an idea of good because He is good.

That's what I would have said that morning if we'd had more time. Remember what I did say? "Jesus is the source of our blessings." I think this sums up having a blessed day even better: "Blessed are those who hunger and thirst for righteousness, for they shall be satisfied" (Matt. 5: 6).

Sincerely, A Friend.

P.S. Have a blessed day!

The Graceful Judge

June 1, 2022

When a world leader invokes God, it stands out. Sometimes, it is political pandering. But it always takes spunk because, after all, God is so controversial.

This time, it was Hungarian Prime Minister Viktor Orban. In a speech to a political gathering, he talked about a philosophy of governance. In a rather pointed remark he said, "If one does not believe that one day (he) will have to answer for his deeds before the Lord God...he (thinks he) can do anything that is in his power." He was suggesting a wise leader is a restrained leader, not unlike the American founders' idea that government answers to the people, and the people to God. It is also not unlike Alexandr Solzhenitsyn's conclusion about Russia's chaos during his lifetime: "Men have forgotten God."

God is controversial if you don't want the world to be like this: "He has established His throne for judgment, and He will judge the world in righteousness" (Psa. 9:7-8). Yet we live in a moral world where what's right, just, and fair punctuate every day (especially if you're raising children!). Each one of us enters the world with a sense of morality along with the inability to keep even our own moral standards, much less God's. He has something to say about idolatry, adultery, honesty, theft, etc. It's easy to stumble at any of these and if you do, you're guilty of all (Jas. 2:10). In this age of ego stroking and participation trophies, it's hard to hear that we are guilty on all counts.

You do understand that's why the truth about Jesus is "good news," right? The God who judges has made a way for you to be blameless, despite your shortcomings. "If God is for us, who is against us? Who will bring a charge against God's elect? God is the one who justifies; Christ Jesus is He who died, yes, rather who was raised, who is at the right hand of God, who also intercedes for us" (Rom. 8:31-34).

The good news is not that difficult to believe. The thief on the cross believed Jesus who said simply, "Today you will be with me in Paradise." Pastor Alistair Begg imagines a dialogue between that man and the angel at heaven's gate.

"What are you doing here?"

"I don't know."

"Are you clear on the doctrine of justification by faith?"

"Never heard of it."

"Then on what basis are you here?"

"All I know is the man on the middle cross said I could come."

That makes me imagine Jesus stepping forward and saying, "All charges are dropped. This one is mine!" (Col. 2:13-14).

Orban is right. God judges. Some may hear that as an attempt to motivate by fear and guilt. But for those who trust Jesus, love and gratitude motivate us to live life God's way. We have reason to welcome the moment we meet that graceful Judge face to face.

Rumspringa

June 8, 2022

Amish fathers let their young adult offspring explore the world outside the boundaries of their faith community. It's a rite of passage.

It's their "rumspringa," which translates "jumping around." It's a time to experience the temptations of living among the "English," to look for a spouse, or decide if they will embrace the faith of their parents. I admire the courage of Amish fathers who release their children to choose between exercising responsible choices or sowing wild oats.

That's not unlike a story Jesus told about a young man who could no longer bear living at home. He demanded and received an inheritance from his father, which he used to fund his rumspringa far from home. When money ran out, he took a job feeding pigs. He was hungry enough to eat the pig food. He knew his father's hired men had it better than him, so he went home to ask his father for a job.

He was willing to endure the humiliation of the whole household seeing him return in such a state. It was an act of repentance after learning the hard lessons of life away from father. How did the father respond? "While he was still a long way off, his father saw him and felt compassion, and ran and embraced him" (Luke 15:20), ignoring the hog pen stench on the son's tattered clothes. The father

149

showed love and forgiveness as he welcomed his son home.

In a way, your life on earth is a rumspringa. The Creator designed the world to have beauty and purpose. But it is also a place you can sow wild oats and live life your way. Life can be harsh as it teases the aroma of happiness while you slog through the muck of pig pens. Life can stink, forcing you to consider what's real, what matters.

How do you respond when life stinks? "We were burdened excessively beyond our strength," Paul writes, "so that we would not trust in ourselves, but in God who raises the dead" (2 Cor. 1:8-9). You have a Heavenly Father who loves you. Come home.

Jastrow's Logic

June 15, 2022

*In the beginning God created
the heavens and the earth. (Gen. 1:1)*

Or did he? Scientists in the 20th century assumed there must be another explanation for the origins of the universe. Many adopted the worldview of materialism, and believed it was their duty to relieve mankind of primitive notions about origins. That's why Edwin Hubble's discovery of the red shift set many scientists on edge. They knew it had theistic implications.

The red shift indicated that stars are moving outward, as the universe continues to expand. As physicist Robert Jastrow explained it, imagine filming this expansion, then running the film in reverse. Eventually all mass, energy, and space would be reduced to a finite singularity, i.e., a beginning called the "Big Bang" in popular parlance.

Jastrow founded NASA's Goddard Institute. He was agnostic about the existence of God. But he didn't mind pointing out the logical, theistic implications of the Big Bang. He calls it "an exceedingly strange development, unexpected by all but the theologians. For the scientist who has lived by his faith in the power of reason, the story ends like a bad dream. He has scaled the mountains of ignorance; he is about to conquer the highest peak; as he pulls himself over the final rock, he is greeted by a band of theologians who have been sitting there for centuries."

One of his contemporaries, Stephen Hawking, posited a mathematical explanation in the field of quantum cosmology as the cause of material world. Those who look for reasons to dismiss the God explanation put their faith in Hawking, who was no doubt a brilliant scientist. But Hawking himself identified the problem with his proofs. He asked, "What is it that breathes fire into the equations and makes a universe for them to describe?" In other words, equations do not create. He may have the right equation, and equations exist in minds. For quantum cosmology to have explanatory power, it needs a mind predating the material world. And that mind had to have the power to breathe fire into it, to make something (the Big Bang) happen!

Jastrow supposed Albert Einstein shared his thoughts about science pointing to God. He quoted Einstein saying, "the harmony of natural law...reveals an intelligence." Jastrow added, "The beauty and simplicity of those laws...suggest a design. A design suggest a designer. That was (Einstein's) back door approach to the question of belief in God."

Here is what theologians know: "In the beginning was the Word...All things came into being through Him...And the Word became flesh and dwelt among us" (John 1). Jesus, God the Son, is that Word. Those who looked into His face saw the One who spoke the universe into existence. Those who believe in Him will not perish but have eternal life (John 3:16). And science keeps pointing us to that same Creator!

The Way Back

June 17, 2022

From Columbine (1999) to Sandy Hook (2012) and now Uvalde, our nation's schoolchildren are under attack by young men. Can we find our way back from this insanity?

Not every problem has a political solution. To be sure, gun control vs. school hardening is a political debate that will continue. But it's a debate about band aids when a tourniquet is needed. It's an illusion to think politics can address the cultural trauma.

An election won't fix this because politics is not the reason young shooters are psychotic, murderous, and suicidal. Chuck Colson often observed that politics is downstream from culture. So, if the problem of mass shootings is not because of political failure, perhaps it is because the culture has lost something.

Psychiatrist and cultural critic Iain McGilchrist says we are losing a sense of belonging and personal security. In The Matter with Things, he lists six ways the culture contributes to that loss. "If you had set out to destroy the happiness and stability of a people," he writes, "it would have been hard to improve on our current formula:

(1) Remove yourself as far as possible from the natural world;

(2) Repudiate the continuity of your culture;

(3) Believe you are wise enough to do whatever you happen to want and not only get away with it, but have a right to it — and a right to silence those who disagree;

(4) Minimize the role played by a common body of belief;

(5) Actively attack and dismantle every social structure as a potential source of oppression; and

(6) Reject the idea of a transcendent set of values."

To help you unpack this formula, think addictive social media and identity confusion. Replace common values with individual preferences, and natural family with transient relationships. Define oppressors by race and sex. Undermine our institutions. Call dissent "hate." And ultimately, exchange that great cornerstone of Western Civilization, Christian faith and morality, for celebration of anything but.

Yet you are not without hope for finding meaning and happiness in this cultural moment. For anyone looking, Jesus said, "I am the way, the truth, and the life" (John 14:6). He offers to connect you to the Father. In that relationship you find wisdom and purpose. Christ is "the power of God and the wisdom of God" (1 Cor. 1:24). You "are His workmanship, created in Christ Jesus for good works" (Eph. 2:10). You are valued, and not here by accident. He has determined your time and location, "that they would seek God...and find Him, though He is not far from each one of us." (Acts 17:27).

The killing of children shouts a culture's failures. Reject the noise and insanity. Believe in and walk with your Savior who loves you. Join your fellow travelers who know the Way.

Proverbs Reader

June 29, 2022

You could use a bit of wisdom today, couldn't you? Take a hint from these bits from the Bible's Proverbs. If the shoe fits...

"The beginning of wisdom is: acquire wisdom" (4:7). Reminds me of Barney Fife. "Here at the Rock we have two rules. Rule number one: obey all rules!" It's wise to seek wisdom. How? "The fear of the Lord is the beginning of wisdom, and the knowledge of the Holy One is understanding" (9:10).

"Do not answer a fool according to his folly, or you will also be like him" (26:4). If you argue with an "information-deprived" person, others can't tell the difference between the two of you.

Know when to keep your mouth shut. "Even a fool, when he keeps silent, is considered wise; when he closes his lips, he is considered prudent" (17:28).

On seduction: "With her flattering lips she seduces him. Suddenly he follows her as an ox goes to the slaughter" (7:21-22). People and thoughts will tempt you with things that do not turn out well. Then there's this: "The ways of a man are before the eyes of the Lord, and He watches all his paths" (5:21).

How to mar beauty: "As a ring of gold in a swine's snout so is a beautiful woman who lacks discretion" (11:22). On the other hand, here is true beauty: "Charm is deceitful and beauty is vain, but a woman who fears the Lord, she shall be praised" (31:30).

Which is better, love or steak? "Better is a dish of vegetables where love is than a fattened ox served with hatred" (15:17). Surely, you'd prefer love! "A friend loves at all times, and a brother is born for adversity" (17:17). Brothers are meant to show love in adversity, not cause it!

Manage your relationships. "A gentle answer turns away wrath, but a harsh word stirs up anger" (15:1). You'll have a nicer life if you manage your own anger. "A hot-tempered man stirs up strife, but the slow to anger calms a dispute" (15:18).

This is funny: "The sluggard says, 'There is a lion in the road!' " (26:13). For some, there's always a reason they can't show up or finish the task. Successful people find ways to get stuff done. The sluggard's excuses can be laughable.

On possessions: You can't take it with you, right? "Better is a little with the fear of the Lord than great treasure and turmoil with it" (15:16). "He who has God and everything else," C. S. Lewis wrote, "has no more than he who has God only."

The best proverbs offer a challenge and a reason to embrace faith. "Trust in the Lord with all your heart and do not lean on your own understanding. In all your ways acknowledge Him, and He will make your paths straight" (3:5-6).

If the shoe fits wear it, and walk on the wise, straight paths.

Find the Anchor

July 6, 2022

"We Make Marines," the sign shouted as I drove beneath it. It was a steel version of a Parris Island drill instructor making sure I got the message.

I was out of my element, and a bit unnerved. The gate sentry made me park within eyesight so he could run a background check. "I'm supposed to be on the access list," I explained. He chuckled. I complied.

Upon my release, I drove through the base to the homes along the waterfront. I was visiting my Auburn roommate from long ago. Captain Terry Gordon, USN, was set to retire after 30 years as a chaplain to Marines and Sailors.

The next day, it took three Marine generals, a letter from George W. Bush, a video message from Charles Barkley, and a Marine band to celebrate Gordon's final bosun's whistle. They also celebrated his family for their support. He traveled the world to advance the Navy's mission. As a chaplain, he advanced the Kingdom of God.

The same day, newly minted U.S. Marines were graduating from 13 weeks of basic training. They had endured separation from their families, physical and mental endurance training, and The Crucible - the final transformation from recruit to Marine.

I couldn't help but notice the contrast. One was looking back over his career. Others were looking forward to theirs. All were transitioning. As are we. Life comes at us in seasons, doesn't it? You are always transitioning, adapting to changes, even while you wish things would stay the same.

Life transitions can be a steady current or a lashing typhoon. Either way, you need something to steady you. By faith in the Lord Jesus Christ, you find God's unchangeable purpose, which is to offer you a hope that accompanies you through life. We "have strong encouragement to take hold of the hope set before us. This hope we have as an anchor of the soul, a hope both sure and steadfast" (Heb. 6:18-19).

Some young Marine recruits did find the anchor of their souls that previous weekend. At a Parris Island chapel service, over 100 of them indicated they wanted a personal faith in Christ. Amen.

The Good Fight

July 13, 2022

"I don't have any idea how I did it," Woody Williams said. PTSD must have something to do with his lack of memory about the day he was in the fight of his life.

It happened in 1945 in the black sands of Iwo Jima. The Marines had trained him as a weapons specialist. When tanks failed to open a lane for the infantry to advance, he volunteered to eliminate a network of concrete pillboxes and mines. Carrying special weapons meant he could not carry a rifle, so four Marines accompanied him.

For four hours, he attacked and returned to replenish his weapons. He faced small arms fire and a bayonet surge. His courage and success allowed his company to reach its objective. Two of his protectors died that day, the same day the Marines raised the American flag on Mount Suribachi. Later that year, President Truman presented Williams the Medal of Honor. He was 21.

Williams was a tormented hero. What he had done in battle and the loss of those two men left him with a burden of guilt. He suffered recurring, fiery nightmares. He had suicidal thoughts. He was in a new fight – to survive his memories. Through all this, he tried to remain self-sufficient. "I didn't need God in my life," he said.

When he was 38, Williams reluctantly attended an Easter service with his family. When the preacher mentioned the sacrifice of the Lord Jesus who takes away sin and guilt, Williams remembered the Marines who sacrificed their lives. He realized his own need. That day he placed his faith in Jesus, the God who sacrificed His life. "That day, my life changed," he said. The nightmares stopped. Turns out he did need God in his life.

Williams had a long career serving his fellow veterans. He served as chaplain of the Medal of Honor Society for 35 years and was not ashamed of his Christian faith. He could say with Paul, "I have fought the good fight, I have finished the course, I have kept the faith. In the future there is laid up for me the crown of righteousness, which the Lord, the righteous Judge, will award to me on that day" (2 Tim. 4:7-8).

What is the good fight? For Williams it was the fight against the guilt of what he had done, of surviving when others didn't. It was confronting selfish pride, which would limit his service to others. Ultimately it is a fight to trust not yourself, but the God who loves, heals, and forgives, the God who grants righteousness to those who believe. "I am not ashamed of the gospel...for in it the righteousness of God is revealed from faith" (Rom. 1:16-17).

Woody Williams, the last living WWII Medal of Honor recipient, left the land of the dying for the land of the living in 2022. He was 98.

Wiping Tears

July 20, 2022

I was recently visiting with a chaplain from the Billy Graham Evangelistic Association-Rapid Response Team. They usually respond with Samaritan's Purse in serving suffering people. Think war (Ukraine), poverty (Haiti), mass casualty (Uvalde), and disease (COVID). He asked me how I would answer the question they hear so often. "Why did God let this happen?"

The "why" question assumes that God exists, which is an important starting point. It also assumes that God is knowledgeable and powerful enough to affect what happens in this world. That implies He is also capable of having reasons for allowing evil to continue for now, reasons that are beyond human understanding.

But He has already done something about it. "If God has willingly suffered death on the cross," Vince Vitale writes, "He has made such an extravagant display of His love for us that it is rational to trust Him, even when we lack full understanding." God identifies with our suffering and meets us in the midst of it. He is the God who is for us even when life makes no sense, and loss seems so random and pointless.

Jesus could have prevented his friend Lazarus from dying. But he didn't, and he wept over it. He explained to Lazarus' sister Martha, "I am the resurrection and the life; he who believes in Me will live even if he dies" (John 11:25). Then he proved it by raising Lazarus from the dead. Tears

161

are part of the journey for now, but by faith in Christ Jesus you will arrive in the place where "He will wipe away every tear from their eyes; and there will no longer be any death; there will no longer be any mourning, or crying, or pain" (Rev. 21:4).

So, with that explanation, here is a short answer to the "why" question. "I cannot say anything that will take away your pain in this moment, nor can I explain why this happened. But you need to know that God loves you and knows what has happened to you. This is the same God that came to earth to endure human suffering just like you. He did that to take away your sin and offer you a home with Him in eternity where there is no suffering. Until then, He will be with you. And He has sent me here to make sure you know that."

BGEA-RRT chaplains and Samaritan's Purse teams wipe tears from the eyes of people whom God loves. You can do the same.

Awesome God

July 27, 2022

Scientists recently launched the James Webb Space Telescope (JWST). Humans can now see deep space like never before. The images are at once beautiful, mysterious, and comforting.

The JWST orbits the sun, unobstructed by earth's atmosphere. The infrared telescope is 21 feet wide and is protected by a tennis court-sized sunshield. "If you held a grain of sand on the tip of your finger at arm's length," Bill Nelson of NASA said about one image, "that is the part of the universe you are seeing."

The JWST will confirm what scientists have known since the 1920s. The universe is expanding, which means it had a beginning. Before that discovery, scientists believed the universe was eternal. "Then there was no need to explain," Simon Singh writes, "how it was created, when it was created, why it was created, or Who created it. Scientists were particularly proud that they had developed a theory of the universe that no longer relied on invoking God." But it didn't hold. It was a futile quest that continues today, despite the evidence for a Creator.

I appreciate the talents of the JWST scientists and engineers. When I see the images, I'm awestruck. God spoke those stars and galaxies into existence in the vast reaches of space. "The worlds were prepared by the word of God, so that which is seen was not made out of things which are visible" (Heb. 11:3). That puts humanity into perspective. In his poem "The Brook," Tennyson reminds us how finite we are.

I murmur under moon and stars in brambly wildernesses.

I linger by my shingly bars, I loiter round my cresses.

And out again I curve and flow to join the brimming river.

For men may come and men may go, but I go on forever.

It's amazing how nature and the night sky bring ultimate questions to mind. It happened to the Psalmist. "When I consider Your heavens, the work of Your fingers, the moon and the stars, which You have ordained; What is man that You take thought of him?" (Psa. 8:3-4).

Within this vast universe, God fine-tuned earth to sustain life. He revealed Himself as Jesus, God the Son, by whom "all things were created in the heavens and on earth" (Col. 2:16). He coded your DNA so you can have a mind to know Him and a conscience to mind Him. In time, He "became flesh and dwelt among us" (John 1:14). Not content to leave you separated from Him by sin, He suffered death "in order to present you before Him holy and blameless and beyond reproach" (Col. 1:22). The invitation is, "whoever believes in Him shall not perish, but have eternal life" (John 3:16). By faith, you are reconciled to the eternal God.

The JWST images reveal the handiwork of the transcendent Creator who knows your name and loves you enough to be your Savior. He is an awesome God!

Jordan Peterson

August 3, 2022

"Young men our age are, honestly, lost. Peterson's book is about what makes you happy through responsibility, meaningfulness, and finding something you truly enjoy." That sentiment from a fan explains the popularity of clinical psychologist Jordan Peterson and his 2018 book, 12 Rules for Life.

Peterson attracts attention because he challenges current cultural ideologies as foolish. He's a secular prophet, calling out for a restoration of truth, common sense, and mutual respect. He makes no claim to religious faith, but that does not stop him from issuing a friendly charge to those who do. "The Christian Church is there to remind people," he says in a video, "young men included, and perhaps even first and foremost, that they have a woman to find, a garden to walk in, a family to nurture, an ark to build, a land to conquer, a ladder to heaven to build, and the utter terrible catastrophe of life to face stalwartly in truth, devoted to love, and without fear."

Peterson appeals to Christians to connect young men to meaning and purpose. I like his reference to the historical narratives in the Hebrew Scriptures. But he may misunderstand building "a ladder to heaven." That is built by God Himself, not by you. Jesus, God the Son, is the ladder, built by His sacrifice on the cross for your sin. Your response to that sacrifice is repentance and faith.

165

Life as a Christian is appealing as an antidote to the "terrible catastrophe of life." To begin with, everybody needs love and a loving community. "Love one another," Jesus said, "even as I have loved you." Christianity also offers freedom from confusion and deception. You can "know the truth and the truth will make you free."

It's a new way to experience life. You sacrifice your old ways to find a new cause to live or die for. "Whoever loses his life for My sake will find it," Jesus said. In Him, you are not only re-created as "a new self," but also join in God's creativity by offering others reasons to embrace and believe the truth.

Jesus' call is, "Follow me!" That is a mystery and an adventure as we walk into the unknown. The Christian life takes courage to stand for what matters. Jesus warned that doing so could attract persecution. But we stand as citizens of the Kingdom of God. The King we worship "is not of this world," but He's still at work in it.

So, allow me to deploy Peterson's turn of phrase in summary. In Christ you have a love to share, a freedom to celebrate, a reason to sacrifice, an opportunity to create, an adventure to experience, a call to courage, and a King to worship. That is how you, young men included, face life as a stalwart follower of Jesus Christ.

(John 8:32, 10:27, 13:34, 15:20, 18:36, Matt. 16:25, Eph. 4:24)

But to Minister

Twin girls born in rural South Georgia during the depression years didn't have many advantages. But someone took the words of Jesus seriously - and impacted generations.

The physician attending their home birth did not believe the tiny babies would survive. But they did, and at age 15 placed first in their high school graduating class. A librarian who was impressed with their potential and knew their circumstances suggested they apply to Berry College.

Martha Berry's life spanned the years from the Civil War to WWII. Moved by the plight of children of poor landowners and tenant farmers, she began a Sunday school class on the family property near Rome, Georgia. That led to her opening first a boarding school for high school education, then Berry College. She offered the opportunity for students to work and earn their tuition, room, and board while receiving an education. She was not offering a handout but rather the dignity of serving others. They farmed, cleaned, and cooked for fellow students and staff.

Berry adopted the motto, "Not to be ministered unto but to minister." This expression is taken from an exchange between Jesus and the sons of Zebedee. They wanted Him to make them privileged leaders. "You do not know what you're asking," He replied. "Whoever wishes to become great among you shall be your servant." That idea is at the core of the Christian gospel. "For even the Son of man (Jesus) came not to be ministered unto, but to minister, and to give His life a ransom for many" (Mark 10:35-45, KJV). Berry took the words of Jesus seriously, and that means a life of sacrifice and service.

In 1950, the teenaged twins took the Nancy Hanks train to Atlanta where they boarded a bus to Rome. Despite intense homesickness, they endured and earned college degrees. One of those girls is my mother. At Berry College, she met my father. With college degrees in hand, the newlyweds began their careers and later their family. Berry's impact to their children and successive generations was not just to elevate their economic class. It was the legacy of service to others, as taught and modeled by our Savior.

Martha Berry never married. She dedicated her treasure, land, and life to serve others. It was a simple gesture when she sat down with a few poor kids to teach them Bible stories. She couldn't have known how that one act of obedience would change not only their lives, but hers as well.

Here is your takeaway. If you want to live a meaningful life and leave a generational legacy as a powerful rejoinder to our era's unapologetic selfishness, then believe and follow Jesus. That means living by His words, "not to be ministered unto but to minister."

Believing Is Seeing

August 17, 2022

Dr. Michael Guillen was the ABC News Science Editor (1988-2002). He earned a rare three-discipline Ph.D. from Cornel in physics, mathematics and astronomy. What he learned as a scientist led him to believe in God and become a Christian. He writes about it in his book, Believing Is Seeing.

Guillen's first belief was in science. While at Cornel, he began to seek answers for universal, ultimate questions. He and fellow student Lauren, also an atheist, looked for answers in the Bible. "It reminded me immediately," he writes, "of what I'd been learning in quantum physics." He explains that quantum physics defies logic but it's not nonsense. "I recognized the possibility that the New Testament was translogical (a truth that's not logical) – like quantum physics it was signaling profundity."

He began to ask specific questions of science and worldview. Does absolute truth exist? Are there truths that cannot be proven? Is the universe designed for life? He found that the atheistic worldview is opposed to science. But despite the popular notion that science contradicts faith, he found that the Christian worldview and science agree on the answers to his questions.

After 20 years of exploring science and world religions, Guillen came to a personal decision, which remained private until a stunning moment on live TV. A panel was discussing Sir Ian Wilmut's cloning of a sheep named

Dolly, and the implications for humans. The show host Charlie Gibson called for final thoughts. "Well, Charlie, I'm concerned that Wilmut's cloning technique might one day be used to clone a human being," Guillen said. "It worries me not just as a scientist, but as a scientist who happens to believe in God." He couldn't believe he just "outed" himself on national television, but the response of his viewers was encouraging.

A near-tragic incident affirmed Guillen's faith. He had joined an expedition to visit the Titanic wreck resting miles below the surface – even though he suffered from hydrophobia (fear of water). As they circled the wreck, a current thrust their vessel into the Titanic's propeller. They were stuck and his phobia began to emerge. Then "something happened that's difficult to describe," he writes. "It was as if an invisible presence had entered the sub. At the same time, an uncanny and unheralded sensation of peace washed over me." After what seemed like an eternity, the pilot freed the sub and they continued on their expedition and returned safely.

Afterwards, Guillen and Lauren (now his wife, also a believer), read these words together: "Where shall I go from your spirit? Or where shall I flee from your presence? If I take the wings of the morning and dwell in the uttermost parts of the sea, even there your hand shall lead me" (Psa. 139). "I experienced that psalm," Guillen remembers, "God's presence and peace, right when I was resigned to kissing my life good-bye."

The Hug

August 24, 2022

"He could have seen me as trying to throw a punch," Isaiah Jarvis said about approaching the mound during a Little League playoff game. But that was not his intention. Not at all.

Kaiden Shelton threw the pitch that hit Isaiah in the head. Isaiah collapsed at the plate, mainly due to the shock. But the ball had glanced off his helmet, and he realized he was not hurt. After he made his way to first base, he noticed the pitcher Kaiden struggling to collect himself. "I see Kaiden getting emotional," Isaiah said, "so I tossed my helmet to the side." He tossed caution to the side also as he approached to the mound...but not to throw a punch. He went to Kaiden a hug saying, "Hey, you're doing great!" He later explained, "I was trying to spread Jesus' love and do what He would do in that situation."

Wow. Think maybe we adults could learn something from "the hug felt 'round the world"? Isaiah's coach Sean Couplen thinks so. He reflected on the incident going viral. "I believe what we are seeing is that our world is tired of divisiveness," he said. "Friendship and caring trump competition."

What you see happening between these young men is a display of empathy. Isn't that part of Jesus' radical ethic, to "treat people the same way you want them to treat you," and "love your neighbor as yourself"? (Matt. 7:12, 22:39)

To do these, you must imagine what people are going through, sense what they feel and need, and react to their concerns. Sometimes more is needed than just a "shake it off," or "he'll get over it."

People are more important than competition. Business can take a lesson here. Making a sale cannot be more important than treating people with fairness, honesty, and integrity. You might want to hold off on the hugs at work though – that might not go over well!

"That's really the main take of all this," Isaiah said about his moment in the spotlight. "Just treat others how you want to be treated." You may not yet embrace the Christian faith but surely you can agree that when it teaches young men to live like this, everyone benefits. Isaiah shows empathy. Be like Isaiah.

The Meaning of Hope

August 31, 2022

When you acquired your first car, started a new job, or first fell in love, you had hope. It wasn't just a car, but an expression of independence. It wasn't just a job, but a better income or career. It wasn't just about a person, but a loving, meaningful relationship.

Yet hope can let you down. Let me take you back to 1971 during the Vietnam War, when John Lennon released the song "Imagine." He imagined "all the people living for today." He hoped away countries, religions, and possessions in order to usher in world peace and eliminate greed and hunger. It was one of the most popular songs of the twentieth century, but it produced nothing for which Lennon hoped. We still yearn for peace and human flourishing.

What's the point of hope when it fails to produce the ideal? How do we make sense of it, when the idea of the thing is better than the thing itself, as happens so often? C. S. Lewis offers answers in <u>Mere Christianity</u>. He uses the examples of marriage, vacations, and learning. Even if the wife is pleasant, the hotels and scenery excellent, and the career in pharmacy interesting, "Something has evaded us," he writes.

He offers three possible responses. The "Fool's Way" is to blame the thing that doesn't fulfill your hopes. Get a new wife or try a more expensive trip and maybe you'll catch this elusive sense of satisfaction that beckons you.

The "Sensible Man" decides that such passions are the idealism of youth. He gives up on hope and resigns himself to boredom and hopelessness.

The third response is the "Christian Way." It understands that humans are born with longings, some of which are fulfilled. But, "If I find in myself a desire which no experience in this world can satisfy," Lewis writes, "the most probable explanation is that I was made for another world." Your unrequited hopes point to something deeper, your true country, which you find by faith in Christ. Such is the meaning of hope.

"I go to prepare a place for you," Jesus said, "and you know the way" (John 14). That's what you are really hoping for, to live in the land of the King who loves you.

Forgiven Debt

September 7, 2022

Forgiveness is in the news. The president decided that the federal government should forgive $10,000 of student loan balances.

I'm not interested here in the politics of that move. I do note how the level of student loans has changed in my lifetime. I graduated from university with a student loan debt equivalent to 40% of my starting salary. That was serviceable. Some time back, I tuned in to a radio call-in program. A young lady wanted advice on paying her student loans. She had recently graduated in graphic arts and landed a job in her field. Her loan was 400% of her starting salary. She needed help. She discovered that she could not manage that level of debt.

How would you feel if you incurred a debt you could not pay? That was the tact Jesus took in answering Peter's question, "How often should I forgive my brother?" True to form, he told a story. A king had a servant who owed more than he could repay in a lifetime. That being the case, the king considered harsh terms against the servant and his family. When the servant pled his case, the king "felt compassion and released him and forgave him the debt."

Jesus' point was that you have no hope to repay your sin debt to God. No one can offend you more than your sin offends a holy God. So, when you consider what it feels like to be forgiven much by God, you have reason to forgive others. How often? As often as you have been forgiven. The servant in the story did not apply this lesson, and the king held him to account for his vindictive ways (Matt. 18:21-35).

How do you incur debt to God that you cannot pay? He created each one of us with a sense of right and wrong, a moral law you might say. Despite your best efforts, you cannot be perfect in keeping that law. You are born that way. "Christianity tells people to repent," C. S. Lewis writes, "and promises them forgiveness. It has nothing to say to people who do not know they have done anything to repent of and who do not feel that they need any forgiveness." You must know just how deep in debt you really are before you can appreciate that God's forgiveness is deeper still.

That young lady I mentioned understood her desperate situation. The radio host offered some predictable suggestions, like look for a better-paying job, move in with her parents, or sell her car. But what if, in the moment she realized what she had gotten herself into, the radio host offered to pay her debt in full? He would be committing his own resources to settle a debt he did not owe, on behalf of someone who had a debt she could not pay. That sounds like what Jesus did.

"In Him we have redemption through His blood, the forgiveness of our trespasses, according to the riches of His grace which He lavished on us" (Eph. 1:7-8).

Pursuit of God

September 14, 2022

A. W. Tozer's <u>The Pursuit of God</u> reveals a pastor's heart. "I want deliberately to encourage this mighty longing after God," he writes. I share his purpose here.

So much competes for our time and focus. In this smart phone and social media age, it's drivel that competes for our attention. The algorithms know what you pursue by keeping up with your clicks and offering you more of the same. When you stop for a minute and take stock, you realize you aren't pursuing your true longings.

Tozer was speaking to believers who know what matters – a relationship with God through Christ Jesus – but do not act as though it is a lifelong pursuit. "The whole transaction of religious conversion has been made mechanical and spiritless," he writes. "The man is 'saved,' but he is not hungry nor thirsty after God." God has revealed Himself to be a Person, and you are made in His image. You can learn what He thinks, desires, enjoys, and loves. He communicates with your soul through the avenues of your mind and emotions. He uses Scripture, prayer, and other believers to intensify your desire for Him. Join the pursuit!

Moses asked, "Let me know Your ways that I may know you," (Exo. 33:13) and that was after he met God on the mountain. David cried out, "Whom have I in heaven but You? And besides You, I desire nothing on earth" (Psa. 73:25). Paul was blunt. "I count all things to be loss in view of the surpassing value of knowing Christ Jesus my Lord" (Phil. 3:8). History tells stories of believers who lived lives of joy amidst sacrifice, consequence despite failings, and focus over distraction because they fanned the flames of desire for God.

Pursuing that desire has a simple result. "The man who has God for his treasure," Tozer writes, "has all satisfaction, all pleasure, all delight...and he has it purely, legitimately, and forever."

"Trust in the Lord and do good; dwell in the land and cultivate faithfulness. Delight yourself in the Lord; and He will give you the desires of your heart" (Psa. 37:3-4).

Save the Queen

September 21, 2022

In 1952, 25-year-old Queen Elizabeth entered Westminster Abbey for her coronation. As she stood by King Edward's Chair, the Archbishop presented her. "God save Queen Elizabeth!" everyone cried out together.

God certainly gave her a long life. She couldn't have predicted that her reign would last 70 years and span such disturbing and tumultuous years. Yet she served her people and the world with grace and endurance. She also served God. Her faith in Jesus inspired her. "The teachings of Christ have served as my inner light," she said recently.

Her 2015 Christmas message came amidst a year of terrorism and migrating refugees. The Chinese communists had made troubling power moves. "It is true that the world has had to confront moments of darkness this year," she said, "but the gospel of John contains a verse of great hope - The Light shines in the darkness, and the darkness has not overcome it." The context is that Jesus is God the Son, the Creator in human flesh who offers the gift of eternal life. "In Him was life, and the life was the Light of men" (John 1:1-5). The Queen was offering the Light that overcomes the darkness of evil.

In 2020, the world was responding to the COVID pandemic. In that year's Christmas message, the Queen mentioned one of Jesus' parables. "This wonderful story of kindness is still relevant today. Good Samaritans have emerged across society showing care and respect for

179

all...reminding us that each one of us is special and equal in the eyes of God." By creating us all in His image, God made the Queen and the pauper of equal and high value. "In the image of God He created him; male and female He created them" (Gen. 1:27). He made you as a unique person so He could love you. When you grasp that God made, values, and loves you, it moves you from selfishness toward loving your neighbor.

The Queen's 1952 coronation service ended with the singing of the anthem, "God Save the Queen." By all indications, He did. And now, Elizabeth has departed for the land of the living. She was 96.

Lay the Burden Down

September 28, 2022

Jack London's <u>The Call of the Wild</u> was required reading in my high school. It is red in tooth and claw. It reveals London's burdensome view that this harsh world is all of reality.

The protagonist of the novel is Buck, a dog. He learns by the "law of club and fang" to be an obedient Klondike sled dog. It's a story of weary labor, deadly retribution, and the struggle to survive. At the end, Buck discovers his owner Thornton and the other dogs dead - killed by indigenous people. He joins a wolf pack living in the wild only to return as the legendary "Ghost Dog" who kills humans.

London's life experiences informed his stories and his worldview. As a child he labored 12 to 18 hours a day at a cannery. As a teenager he sailed with a sealing expedition, bludgeoning and skinning seals for days on end. His time in the Klondike damaged his health. He experienced hunger, homelessness, and a stint in the penitentiary. His mother attempted suicide. His birth father denied paternity and suggested any number of other men could be the father.

London's faith was in Darwin. He declared, "I believe that with my death I am just as much obliterated as the last mosquito you and I squashed." A few months before he died at age 40 of an overdose, London explained his credo. "I would rather that my spark should burn out in a brilliant blaze than it should be stifled by dry rot. The proper function of man is to live, not to exist. I shall not waste my days in trying to prolong them." If anything, he lived as though to shorten them. "The ultimate word," he wrote, "is I Like," expressed in his wild adventures, riotous living, and substance abuse. Those were his attempts to offload the burden of living in a pitiless and pointless world.

His is a story of tragedy, not redemption. He missed the evidence all around him of a far greater and more attractive reality – the rest of the story. Even amidst tooth and claw, creation points to something beautiful and sublime. "O Lord, how many are Your works! In wisdom You have made them all; the earth is full of Your possessions. There is the sea, great and broad... animals both small and great. Let the glory of the Lord endure forever. As for me, I shall be glad in the Lord" (Psa. 104).

What is your story? You don't have to live a burdened life, denying that transcendent, eternal good exists. "Come to me, all you who are weary and burdened, and I will give you rest," Jesus said. "Take my yoke upon you and learn from me, for I am gentle and humble in heart, and you will find rest for your souls" (Matt. 11:28-29).

On Curiosity

October 5, 2022

"The important thing is not to stop questioning," Albert Einstein said. "Curiosity has its own reason for existing. One cannot help but be in awe when he contemplates the mysteries of eternity, of life, of the marvelous structure of reality." The reality of the natural world has fewer mysteries thanks to Einstein's curiosity.

Einstein connected curiosity (a state of mind) and questioning (acting on that state of mind). An unasked question is an unanswered one that abandons you on the island of ignorance. That is a desolate place to be, given the mysteries of eternity, life, and reality as Einstein said.

Dr. Sy Garte, an American biochemist, is another curious scientist. Garte was raised to believe in Darwin and Marx. But as a young man, he found those philosophies contradictory. If humans are meaningless products of evolution, he wondered, how did the socialist goals of advancing human dignity make sense? If Christianity is so bankrupt, why was the civil rights movement led by Christians?

Garte pursued an academic career and became a professor. For a while, he accepted the claims of scientism, which holds that science is sufficient for any knowledge humans might need. But being curious, a question began to nag him. Does science hold the keys to unlock ALL mysteries? The answer from the science of quantum mechanics is that some things are unknowable. That led to other questions. Where did the universe come from? How did life begin? What does it mean to be a human being? How did humans develop an ability to create and appreciate art, poetry, music, and humor? His worldview had no satisfactory answers.

Garte tells his story in Christianity Today magazine. His curiosity led him to read the story of Jesus in the Bible, which he found beautiful and believable. Then this rational, sane, and well-educated man had a kind of epiphany. He had an intense vision of himself as a preacher, appealing to a large crowd and saying things he had yet to affirm or even hear before. He began to listen to what the preacher (himself) was saying. His response was emotional, and his heartfelt words flowed. "I believe, and I am saved," he said out loud. "Thank you, Lord Jesus Christ."

Today Garte works with the American Scientific Affiliation helping people who are curious about the link between science and theology. He seems well-positioned to do just that, given his story.

Are you curious? Jesus offers some questions to help you along. "What do you seek?" (John 1:38). "Whom do you seek?" (John 18:7). "Who do you say that I am?" (Mark 8:29). And my favorite, "Everyone who lives and believes in Me will never die. Do you believe this?" (John 11:26). Do you seek answers to the questions of life and eternity? I guess it depends on your curiosity.

The Torrent Burst

October 12, 2022

Many people in our mountain village have friends or family affected by Hurricane Ian. The damage and casualty reports from Florida and South Carolina are disturbing. This is an opportunity for people of faith to love our neighbors, some of whom escaped only with their lives.

The mountains are not immune to hurricanes. No storm surge happens at elevation 2000 feet, but high winds do. In 1995, Opal swept across North Georgia downing trees and powerlines. In 2018, we had wind damage from Michael.

That calls to mind a remarkable post-Michael image from Mexico Beach, FL. The 160 mph winds and 14 ft deep storm surge destroyed over 800 homes and buildings. One aerial image shows a solitary home standing intact along a devasted beach front. Dr. Lebron Lackey built the home to a higher standard than the local building codes - deeper foundations, stronger building materials, and a floodproof design. He expected the house to face a storm like Michael someday.

That's not a bad approach to building a beach home. It's a great approach to life. Just as beach and mountain will face the torrents of weather, you can expect to face adversity in this life. That's reality. You can spend your life simply hoping nothing bad happens, or you can prepare as though it will.

Jesus offers the way to prepare. "Everyone who comes to Me and hears My words and acts on them," He said, "I will show you whom he is like: he is like a man building a house, who dug deep and laid a foundation on the rock; and when a flood occurred, the torrent burst against that house and could not shake it, because it had been well built" (Luke 6:47-48). What were His words meant for you to act on? Love your enemy. Turn the other cheek. Treat others the way you want to be treated. "The good man out of the good treasure of his heart," Jesus summarized, "brings forth what is good" (Luke 6:45).

Adversity is your opportunity to bring forth good from a good heart. But wait! "Only God is good," Jesus said. "The heart is more deceitful than all else," Jeremiah declared. True, so you'll need a source for a new heart that's good: "If anyone is in Christ, he is a new creature," (2 Cor. 5:17). Through faith in the Lord Jesus and by his grace, you have a new perspective, a new heart.

Here's the point. With a new heart set right with God, you build resilience by hearing and acting on the words of Jesus. You know life on this earth is not all of reality, nor does adversity have the final say. You rise above it as a loving, trusting, secure man or woman of God, and are not shaken when the torrent bursts against you.

Courage and Sacrifice

October 19, 2022

Show me a life of purpose and meaning, and I'll show you the character traits of courage and sacrifice. Note that these traits exist only in the presence of adversity.

While recuperating from a war injury, Andrew van der Bijl read a Bible to pass the time. That led him to believe in Christ Jesus. In the early cold war years, he began to smuggle Bibles into communist countries. That's when his associates began to call him "Brother Andrew."

Once, he stopped his Volkswagen in a line of cars at the Romanian border. He watched for hours as the guards ransacked the vehicles in front of him. After praying for a miracle, in a counter-intuitive move he placed some Bibles out in the open. Then it was his turn. He pulled the car forward and stopped. The guard glanced at his passport and waved him through, only to stop the next car and resume the ransacking. From that experience Andrew learned to pray, "Lord, You made blind eyes see. Now make seeing eyes blind."

Over the decades Andrew's ministry changed, but it always involved staring down adversity with courage and sacrifice. In recent years, he built relationships with leaders in the Muslim world, including some in Hamas. He spoke about Christ with them and prayed for them. "We know you love us because you come when no one else will," one told him. The leader of Islamic Jihad sent a cryptic note after one visit. "I pray that God will give us the possibility to unite with you and the Christ." Perhaps he had a life-changing dream about Jesus, as is widely reported among Muslims.

In Andrew's mind, he only did what all Christians do – follow Jesus in the unique ways He calls us. "The Bible is full of ordinary people," Andrew said, "who went to impossible places and did wondrous things simply because they decided to follow Jesus." He rightly believed that every believer is called. "The real calling is not a certain place or career but to everyday obedience. And that call is extended to every Christian, not just a select few."

This is in keeping with Jesus' explanation of the ordinary Christian life. "If anyone wishes to come after Me, he must deny himself, and take up his cross daily and follow Me. For whoever wishes to save his life will lose it, but whoever loses his life for My sake, he is the one who will save it. For what is a man profited if he gains the whole world, and loses or forfeits himself?" (Luke 9:23-25).

Brother Andrew's work attracted like-minded people and continues as a ministry called Open Doors. He found purpose and meaning from a life of courage and sacrifice. In September 2022, he departed for the land of the living. He was 94.

Self-Awareness

October 26, 2022

OK class, our lesson today is self-awareness. Let me show you some ways it might show up, or not. Then we'll get personal.

Jerry Seinfeld is the master of observational comedy. Once, he was thinking about his role in a wedding. "Pretty good title, I thought ... 'Best man.' I thought it was a bit much. I thought we had the groom and the 'pretty good man.' That's more than enough. If I am the best man, why is she marrying him?" Seinfeld's self-awareness is funny!

On rare occasions, self-awareness shows up in politics. A woman politician, Tulsi Gabbard, came to a clarifying realization. She decided to disassociate from a group of people she believes lacks self-awareness. "It is the height of hypocrisy," she said, "for those who claim to be champions for women over decades to deny that there is such a thing as a woman." Her self-awareness led to action.

Here's an example from my (other) profession as a civil engineering consultant. A group of homeowners invited me to discuss options for their failed dam. The lake was a mud bowl, and the state regulators were bearing down. For the first 20 minutes we stood on the dam while one guy's mouth was a flowing pipe with no shutoff valve. They wanted to hear from me, but he wanted to hear himself. He was completely oblivious that he was wasting everyone's time. I finally said, "Sir, you need to switch from

189

transmit to receive. If you want to hear from me, you must stop talking."

And yes, I'm guilty, too. Not long ago I had one of those days that makes you feel harassed and unproductive. Rather than checking it all at the threshold, that evening I got snippy with the missus. It wasn't her fault. I lacked self-awareness. She has her own story, too. Once she did lunch with friends only for one of them to complain, "I just don't have any friends." Ouch.

Jesus did lunch at Simon's house, only for the host to become critical of a certain sinful woman. Jesus told him a story about two debtors. One owed much and the other owed little. The lender forgave both loans. "Which of them will love him more?" He asked. "The one he forgave more," Simon answered. Jesus' point was that host could learn something from this woman if he were more self-aware about his own sinfulness. "Her sins, which are many, have been forgiven, for she loved much, but he who is forgiven little, loves little" (Luke 7).

This is the personal part. The more self-aware you are about your need for forgiveness from a holy God, the more you love Him for taking the penalty of your sin on the cross. Self-awareness makes you a happier and more likeable person. It also makes you a more steadfast and loving follower of Jesus.

A Wondrous Thing

November 2, 2022

It was a wondrous thing to behold! It wasn't just what we saw and heard, but the meaning of it.

The Sons of Jubal came to our town (thanks FBC Blairsville!). Jubal Brass accompanied the men's chorus. Over 200 musicians filled the stage. The Truett McConnell (University) Chorale joined them. The auditorium overflowed with young and young-at-heart.

The meaning of the event is found in this: "Let the word of Christ richly dwell within you, with all wisdom teaching and admonishing one another with psalms and hymns and spiritual songs, singing with thankfulness in your hearts to God" (Col. 3:16). Whether it's two or three, or hundreds gathered, music is a way for the word of Christ to dwell within you. The message of this evening concert was that God is holy and worthy of worship. Jesus is the Savior who died for your sins, the Good Shepherd who cares for your soul.

They invited the audience to participate in worship by joining in the singing. We voiced the lyrics, "The work is finished, the end is written, Jesus Christ my living hope!" I was not familiar with the song, but it was becoming easier to follow with the lyrics projected and the chorus leading the way. The words began to settle in my soul. As we came to this verse, it moved me to hear those aging saints, with more years in their past than in their future, singing with confidence:

Hallelujah, praise the one who set me free!
Hallelujah, death has lost its grip on me!
Jesus Christ, my living hope"
("Living Hope," Wickham/Johnson).

C. S. Lewis described Christian musicians as "the most enviable of men; privileged while mortals to honor God like angels and, for a few golden moments, to see spirit and flesh, delight and labour, skill and worship, the natural and the supernatural, all fused into that unity they would have had before the Fall." I think that's his way of saying skilled musicians bring heaven down to earth for a moment. When music is aligned with the word of Christ, that is a meaningful and wondrous thing to behold.

True Empathy

November 9, 2022

Cringeworthy. That's one way to characterize the statements of certain people in the news. They could use some empathy.

Kanye West (now known as "Ye") is a wealthy rap artist. During the last election he announced a presidential bid, naming Kim Kardashian and Elon Musk as his chief advisors. This month he tweeted he was "going death con 3 on Jewish people." He has publicly disclosed his bipolar disorder, but that doesn't make his statements less cringeworthy.

John Fetterman is clearly not well yet. He is the current Lt. Gov. of Pennsylvania, running for U.S. Senate. Five months after suffering a stroke, he's on the debate stage on live TV despite his auditory processing issues. He opens with, "Hi, goodnight everybody." Despite his previous support of a moratorium on fracking he says, "I do support fracking. And I don't, I don't..." I admire his courage. His doctor says he's fit to serve, but...cringeworthy.

Make no mistake. To cringe at verbal gaffs is not the same as empathy, an emotional competency the world could use more of these days. Empathy figures large in the Christian worldview. "Love your neighbor as yourself," Jesus said. The good news is you can learn empathy.

Empathy is connecting with someone's feelings and thoughts and being willing to intervene. Jesus shows us how it's done. When He encounters the widow from Nain in the funeral procession for her only son, he connects with her grief. He touches the coffin and gives her a reason not to weep (Luke 7:14). You may not raise the dead, but you can raise your awareness of what someone is feeling in the moment. Only then can you know if there is more you can do to intervene. The mistake is to make it about you. "Yeah, I've been there. Here's what happened to me..." is not the best way to connect.

You may be less familiar with cognitive empathy, an awareness of someone's thoughts. It didn't take a miracle for Jesus to know his disciples' thoughts. Each wanted an important role in Jesus' earthly ministry and were openly arguing about it. He calls over a child to make his point. "The one who is least among all of you, this is the one who is great" (Luke 9:48). Empathy connects thoughts to truth. But first you must understand what someone is thinking. Empathy removes the shade of deception from the light of truth.

Finding something cringeworthy takes no investment of energy. But empathy is personal, and it costs something to care and take action. It certainly cost Jesus to have empathy for you. "While we were yet sinners, Christ died for us" (Rom. 5:8). He didn't just look through a holy lens and cringe at your predicament. He committed the greatest act of love ever recorded in history. To sacrifice for others, friend, is true empathy.

Clear Thinking

November 16, 2022

Do you consider yourself a thinker? Neuroscientists say your brain processes far more unconscious thoughts than conscious. So, you may not even be aware of what you are thinking or why. You may not be thinking clearly.

Cognitive bias is another term for fast-thinking shortcuts. The human brain is lazy and prefers to seek patterns rather than doing the hard work of processing new information and re-evaluating prior conclusions. Modern neuroscience seeks to understand this phenomenon, but it's always been part of the human experience.

We can see it in Jesus' ministry 2000 years ago. On one particular occasion He encountered confirmation bias (interpreting information in a way that supports your prior beliefs). In a demonstration of divine power, He made a blind and mute man see and speak. The crowds were amazed. But some weren't. They reinterpreted what they saw with their own eyes saying, "This man casts out demons only by Beelzebul, ruler of the demons." Despite what they saw with their own eyes, they still refused to believe Jesus is God the Son. Jesus pointed out the illogic saying, "Any house divided against itself will not stand" (Matt. 12:22-29). So, what evidence would change your doubt about Jesus into faith? Think about it. You have everything to gain.

Jesus also encountered the anchoring bias (relying only on the first information you receive). After He fed thousands of people with five loaves and two fish, some followed Him because they were anchored to the free food. "You seek Me," Jesus said, "because you ate of the loaves and were filled." He tried to get them to move beyond that. "I am the bread of life," He said. "Everyone who beholds the Son and believes in Him will have eternal life" (John 6). So, are you anchored to incomplete first impressions? Don't be anchored to the pain a Christian or a church may have caused you – truth is not limited to human failings. Don't be anchored to the presence of evil in the world – you experience God's love and goodness when you accept His offer of a new identity in Christ.

Another cognitive bias is the bandwagon effect. That's agreeing with what everyone else believes, i.e., going along with the crowd. In His home synagogue, Jesus read a powerful prophecy about the promised Messiah (Isa. 61) then said, "Today this scripture has been fulfilled in your hearing" (Luke 4:21). The crowd became so enraged believing he had committed blasphemy that they tried to throw Him down a cliff. Just because lots of folks agree doesn't make it true. "The way is narrow that leads to life," Jesus said, "and few find it." (Matt. 7:14).

Honest thinkers analyze their thoughts for biases and premature conclusions. They don't mind being in the minority. When it comes to answering ultimate questions about God, faith, eternal destiny, and yourself, don't be victimized by cognitive bias. Use your God-given ability to think clearly.

Thanks for Everything

November 23, 2022

In everything give thanks; for this is God's will for you in Christ Jesus. (1 Thes. 5:18)

The Reader's Digest chronicles the stories of people who shared a life-changing experience, but never knew each other. Here are their stories.

Holly Winter was planning a reunion trip with some of her friends. They planned to surprise a college classmate in his office. But Holly's mom decided to visit her on the same day, disrupting Holly's plans. Crystal Brown-Tatum was engaged and accepted a job in her fiance's city. But things took a turn, so she broke the engagement and decided not to move.

George Keith's story is about his car, which was too new to have transmission trouble. He made an appointment at the dealer for the next morning. After waiting for an hour for a simple repair, he rushed toward the office hoping not to be late for his morning meeting. At least he had a job. Laura Gelman lost hers. Her usual morning commute would have taken her through a certain subway station, but not on this day.

What connects these people? All four would have been in the World Trade Center on September 11, 2001. That is the life-changing experience they share. They live to tell about it. They have a reason to be thankful for an imposing mom, a broken engagement, new car troubles, and a lost job. It's sobering to realize that life's disruptions can actually be a blessing, though we may never know how. But that is one reason to practice what the Bible says, "In everything give thanks" (1 Thes. 5:18).

Consider some of Jesus' encounters with people. From the perspective of eternity, the one leper from the ten should be thankful for the disease because he experienced Jesus' saving power. The man blind from birth should be thankful because the works of God was displayed in him. Lazarus should be thankful that he endured death because many people witnessed and believed in the Resurrection and the Life because of it. And there we are at the foot of the cross, witnesses to the horror and injustice of Jesus's death, with hands raised in gratitude because it means "that we would be holy and blameless before Him" (Eph. 1:4).

"The giving of thanks to God for all His blessings should be one of the most distinctive marks of the believer in Jesus Christ," writes Billy Graham. "We must not allow a spirit of ingratitude to harden our heart and chill our relationship with God and with others." For the believer, life's disruptions cannot change the ultimate truth that we are meant for another place, which Jesus went to prepare for us. And we know the Way. That thought chases away the spirit of ingratitude.

You have much to be thankful for, including eternal life by faith in Christ. Knowing this world is not all of reality is the eternal perspective that makes giving thanks in everything your distinct privilege.

Politics and Religion

November 30, 2022

I'm old enough to remember when politics was seasonal, returning from time to time to disabuse us of our comfortable obliviousness. Now, primary, general, and runoff elections join local, state, mid-term, and presidential elections into a continuous stream of consciousness polluted by fear narratives.

Don't get me wrong. Politics matters. Do your duty and vote! Support your candidate and your cause! It's a citizen's responsibility in our democratic republic. That said, let's touch the third rail and mix politics and religion.

If you think about it, both politics and religion address change - what should or should not change. Political consultants and modern media use fear of the wrong kind of change to get more eyeballs, clicks, or votes. Here is my caution: Do not give in to political fear or go all in for political hope.

French philosopher Jacques Ellul warned denizens of the 20th century about politics becoming the ultimate source of power, hope, and change. Anyone who disagrees "is the true heretic of our day," he writes. "And society excommunicates him as the medieval church excommunicated the sorcerer...This shows us that man in his entirety is being judged today in relation to political affairs, which are invested with ultimate value." Today the culture still values political identity, and also looks for an "intersectionality" of multiple identities to measure your worth.

For the believer, the totality of your identity is Christ. "It is no longer I who live, but Christ lives in me" (Gal. 2:20). That is something that does not change. "Jesus Christ is the same yesterday and today and forever" (Heb. 13:8). The cultural and political ground may move beneath you, but "on Christ the solid rock I stand" the hymn says.

Remember the providence of God and His eternal perspective. "You, Lord, in the beginning laid the foundation of the earth, and the heavens are the works of your hands. They will perish but you remain" (Heb. 1:10-11). Our hope is in God who accomplishes His eternal purposes for this world and its nations, despite elections. "The king's heart is like channels of water in the hand of the Lord. He turns it wherever He wishes" (Prov. 21:1).

Jesus said you are in the world, but not of the world (John 17:11,14). You are a citizen of heaven, so you have no reason to fear the outcome of earthly politics. "The Lord is my light and my salvation; Whom shall I fear?" (Psa. 27:1). Elections happen and you might be stunned at what's changed, but the Lord is neither surprised nor deterred.

There you have it - politics and religion. Elections matter, but heaven's citizens have other ways to catalyze change. Now join me in praying, "Thy Kingdom come, Thy will be done on earth as it is in heaven." Amen.

Advent Vulnerability

December 7, 2022

The CDC issued a Level 2 Alert about a new outbreak of Ebola in Uganda. You may recall the Ebola plague of 2014 in Liberia. During that outbreak, Dr. Kent Brantly was serving in a hospital in Liberia with Samaritan's Purse. Because of his love and dedication, he chose to stay and face the risk of treating infected people. But despite his meticulous attention to safety protocols, he contracted the disease. He received an experimental treatment and eventually recovered at Emory Hospital in Atlanta. To Dr. Brantly, love means being vulnerable.

Vulnerability is not the same as weakness. "The world does not understand vulnerability," writes Brennan Manning. "Neediness is rejected as incompetence and compassion is dismissed as unprofitable. The great deception is that being poor, vulnerable, and weak is unattractive." George Bailey expressed his need in the movie "It's A Wonderful Life." He prayed, "Dear Father in heaven. I'm at the end of my rope. Show me the way." That is raw vulnerability. What happened next changed his life. Then he prayed, "Please God. Let me live again!"

Christmas recalls the historic moment when God became as vulnerable as a baby. The Word became flesh and embraced the risk of the human condition, but not just to teach truth. He made Himself vulnerable to death on the cross to pay the penalty for your sin. Why do that? "For God so loved the world, that He gave His only begotten

201

Son, that whoever believes in Him shall not perish, but have eternal life" (John 3:16). To God, love means being vulnerable.

It takes courage and sacrifice to be vulnerable, whether facing risk, admitting need, or telling the truth. For you, being vulnerable may never mean fighting Ebola in Africa. It does mean loving someone enough to own your mistakes, to admit your contribution to the situation. It means loving God enough to confess your need.

In a mysterious, joyful moment, our Savior who is Christ the Lord, was born for you. Your response is to trust Him for what you need most - forgiveness and a renewed life. Could you be so vulnerable this Advent season?

True Light

December 14, 2022

We who never suffered the malady of blindness take sunsets, children's faces, and everyday tasks for granted. Imagine living in darkness of not seeing, then having the surgical bandages removed!

William, a Liberian man, is a husband and father of four. He suffered blindness for three years and was unable to provide for his family. Remembering when he first heard of a Samaritan's Purse eye surgery team in Monrovia he said, "I was filled with hope for the future." He had the procedure and it worked. "I can read again!" he exclaimed. "I can begin to fish again and send my daughters to school." With bandages off, he had new life.

Stories and metaphors of seeing and light are a well-trodden path to discerning the things of God. Centuries before Christ the prophet wrote, "The people who walk in darkness will see a great light" (Isa. 9:2). Darkness yet looms because evil persists in our world. But we have hope! History confirms the prophet's words. "The true Light which, coming into the world, enlightens every man. He was in the world, and the world was made through Him, and the world did not know Him" (John 1:9-10). The Light is the Creator, entering His creation lying in a manger.

The world suffers with (a sometimes willing) blindness. But people are enlightened by the truth about Jesus. As that great theologian Hank Williams crooned, "I wandered so aimless, life filled with sin. I wouldn't let my dear Savior in. Then Jesus came like a stranger in the night. Praise the Lord, I saw the light!" The bandages are off!

To believe in the true Light is to reflect it. "Every Christian is part of the dust-laden air which shall radiate the glowing epiphany of God, catch and reflect his golden Light," writes Evelyn Underhill. "Ye are the light of the world – but only because you are enkindled, made radiant by the one Light of the world. And being kindled, we have got to get on with it, be useful." Your light is not meant to be hidden under a bushel, Jesus said. "Let your light shine before men" (Matt. 5:16).

Each Christmas we celebrate the Light that pushes back the darkness. It's our annual reminder that wars, hurricanes, and pandemics do not have the last say. It's your reminder that whatever darkness this year has wrought in your life, the true Light appeared in your world to forgive and give life.

That makes Advent a season of hope and anticipation. To celebrate the coming of the Christ Child long ago is to anticipate His return. As surely as the prophet Isaiah got it right, Jesus will fulfill His own promise to return. Until that second Advent, we rejoice because we see eternity just over the horizon. Look! I see that wondrous glow in the eastern sky even now!

The Nativity

December 21, 2022

Two figures, bundled against the stiff cold, shuffle past the streetlight. "Only college students go out on a night like this for coffee," Joan said, glancing at her friend Kara. "Well, only college students are crazy enough," Kara said, "to wait to the last minute to finish their assignments, then need a java to make the final push!"

The young ladies laugh, hoping the distracting moment of truth would help ward off the cold. There's another bit of chill, which they have been avoiding. Joan brought her Christian faith with her to college. She had invited Kara to the Christmas program at her church scheduled for the weekend before finals. "That's the last thing on my mind. No thanks!" Kara had said. She was content to leave any thoughts about God back home.

Joan still felt the sting of Kara's rejection. She, too, had other things on her mind, not uncommon for a first-year student. Was she at the right school, in the right major? Would the student loan debt be worth it? Would she fit in? Would her classmates dismiss her small-town ways as quaint? Those are the thoughts that can push childhood traditions aside. But Joan knew her faith had something to say about her future and who she would be, now that she is on her own. That's why she found being with fellow believers in church comforting, familiar. Why wouldn't she share that with her new friend?

205

They continued along the downtown sidewalk in silence, anxious to huddle over a steamy brew and a warm blueberry scone. They were approaching that church near the coffee shop, the one with the tiny front yard squeezed between two old, red brick store buildings. Kara remembered Joan's invitation. "You know, I'm sorry I responded that way when you brought up the Christmas program. It's just that, well, I don't know what I believe anymore. I just want to focus on finishing the semester."

"I understand," Joan said. "I just thought it would be a welcome break for you. Besides, if I care, I should want the best for you, not just in academics, right?" Kara felt a bit put upon, but she knew Joan was sincere.

"I'll be honest with you," Kara said. "I don't know if God is really there. I mean there's so much pain and darkness in the world. If he is there, why doesn't he do something about it?" Joan wasn't prepared to answer that, so she prayed for insight. To hear such transparency from her friend was a gift.

They neared the church. It was hard not to notice. The church had placed a simple nativity scene in the yard, well-lit by floodlamps. Joan caught Kara's hand and stopped. "There's your answer!" She pointed to the child in the manger. "He did do something about it."

He will wipe away every tear from their eyes; and there will no longer be any death; there will no longer be any mourning, or crying, or pain (Rev. 21:4).

A Lighter Burden

December 28, 2022

What will the new year hold? One thing is for sure - it will be different than the past year. I don't know about you, but I'd like to travel lighter this coming year.

Let's stipulate that 2022 delivered dispiriting events on the national and world scene. If those burdens weren't enough, you have your own freight to carry. Life can make you feel deserted, hurt, lonely, or hopeless. Your burdens only intensify if you marginalize the God of the universe. Life's burdens are evidence for this piece of theology: This is a fallen world, enslaved to corruption (Rom. 8:21). The good news is that you can travel lighter.

Tennyson expressed that yearning with these verses:
Ring out the old, ring in the new.
Ring, happy bells, across the snow,
the year is going, let him go.
Ring out the false, ring in the true.
Ring out false pride in place and blood,
the civic slander and the spite.
Ring in the love of truth and right.
Ring in the common love of good.

These sentiments from 1850 express the cry of our hearts today.

People who travel heavy with burdens rightly yearn for the new, the good, the true. It's true that that life is less about what happens and more about how you react to it. You can manage the burdens you carry. To that end I offer three truths, actually blessings, which will help you travel lighter in the new year.

1. You are valuable to God. He made you in His image and renews you by faith in Christ Jesus. It is, as C. S. Lewis wrote, "almost incredible and only possible by the work of Christ, that any of us who really chooses, shall find approval, shall please God. (You are) loved by God...delighted in as an artist delights in his work." If God is for you, who can be against you (Rom. 8:31)?

2. Your life has meaning. Having a central organizing purpose for life is your reason to stand strong. The highest and most sublime purpose is not to possess things, but to know God. "I count all things as loss," Paul wrote, "in view of the surpassing value of knowing Christ" (Phil. 3:8). To know God is to have meaning.

3. You are created for community. Poet John Donne tells us, "No man is an island." There's a reason the Bible emphasizes loving your neighbor. Shared burdens are lighter. With whom are you living life? Are you sharing the journey with other travelers?

Prepare for the new year by embracing what's right and true. Lighten your burden by receiving these three blessings from God. As Isaac Watts wrote,

No more let sins and sorrows grow,
nor thorns infest the ground.
He comes to make His blessings flow
far as the curse is found.

Scripture References

Index

215